The Ministry
of Law
in the
Church Today

The Ministry
of Law
in the
Church Today

Kevin E. McKenna

UNIVERSITY OF NOTRE DAME PRESS
Notre Dame, Indiana

Copyright 1998 by
University of Notre Dame Press
Notre Dame, IN 46556
All Rights Reserved
Manufactured in the United States of America

The author and publisher are grateful for permission from the
Canon Law Society of America to quote from its publications.

Nihil Obstat
Rev. William F. Laird, J.C.L.
censor deputatus

Imprimatur
†Matthew H. Clark
Bishop of Rochester
8 May 1998

Library of Congress Cataloging-in-Publication Data
McKenna, Kevin E., 1950–
The ministry of law in the church today / Kevin E. McKenna.
p.   cm.
Includes bibliographical references and index.
ISBN 0-268-01441-8 (alk. paper). — ISBN 0-268-01442-6 (pbk. :
alk. paper)
1. Canon law.   I. Title.
LAW
262.9'4—dc21   98-38658

∞ *The paper used in this publication meets the minimum requirements of the*
American National Standard for Information Sciences—Permanence of
Paper for Printed Library Materials, ANSI Z39.48-1984.

To My Parents

Contents

Preface

AS A PRIEST GRADUATE STUDENT STUDYING CANON LAW
in Rome in the early 1980s, it was not uncommon for me to be good-
naturedly teased by other American graduate students in other
disciplines about the "dark side of the Good News." Even after completing my graduate studies and beginning work in our diocesan
office, I have often found myself myself chided by colleagues and
fellow pastoral ministers about my involvement in a field of work
that seems so anachronistic, or, at times, according to some, almost
antithetical to the Gospel itself. When he returned from a retreat
he had conducted in another diocese, even my own bishop (himself
a canon lawyer), smilingly shared a new term that he had heard
while there to describe canon law: "the arteriosclerosis of the Mysti-
cal Body"!

However, for the last several years canon law practitioners have
been working, for the most part behind the scenes, to help provide a
smooth adjustment to the various structures and procedures of the
Church that have been modified as a result of the Second Vatican
Council and its new theological insights. Perhaps the most dramatic
developments, yet to be fully realized and appreciated, are the array
of rights (as well as obligations) that have been formalized and legislated by the 1983 *Code of Canon Law*. The fact that all Christian
faithful have the right to make known their needs and desires to their
pastors, to manifest their opinions on matters which pertain to the
good of the Church, and to receive assistance from their pastors
out of the Church's spiritual gifts—along with several other rights—
clearly shows that the newest code has great potential for significantly and positively affecting the ecclesial community. What
remains problematic is how such rights may be effectively realized
and implemented. An initial and crucial component will be an educational process in which all Catholics come to know about their

rightful status in the Church and what justice demands concerning their participation in the life of the Church by virtue of baptism.

Canon lawyers will continue to talk among themselves about the possible roles of the Church's law in helping to realize the wonderful vision given by the Second Vatican Council. But it's also time now to open this discussion to the wider faith community. So I offer this book as one small contribution to that wider discussion.

I would like to express my gratitude to Bishop Matthew Clark who first invited me, several years ago, to pursue graduate studies in the "dark side" of the Good News. I am also grateful to the priests, deacons, and various pastoral ministers of the Diocese of Rochester who have encouraged me to reflect on many issues in the field of canon law by their excellent questions, problems, and comments. I owe a great debt of gratitude to Dr. Mary Sullivan, R.S.M., faculty member at Rochester Institute of Technology, who patiently and diligently reviewed the manuscript and made many helpful corrections to the text. I owe a debt as well to Dr. Michel Thériault, professor of canon law at St. Paul University in Ottawa, who likewise assisted by making many helpful suggestions. To these and the many others who either directly or indirectly assisted in this effort, I am truly grateful.

Introduction

Q: What do you do when your attorney is up to his neck in sand?
A: Look for more sand.
Q: What's brown and looks good on a lawyer?
A: A Doberman pinscher.
Q: What happens when a lawyer becomes a godfather?
A: He makes you an offer you can't understand.[1]

A POPULAR PASTIME FOR MANY AMERICANS THE LAST FEW years has been sharing jokes about lawyers and the American legal system. Among many possible interpretations, such humor could indicate that at this point the profession and the legal system do not enjoy great popularity or even trust among the American people.

This is particularly sobering in a society which has traditionally upheld law as one of the cherished icons of a vital democracy. Fingers of blame can be pointed in several directions to discover the source of the predicament. In a recent book one lawyer, Philip Howard, claims that the mentality of "over-regulation," so characteristic of our times, has tarnished the perception of law in the United States today.[2] Howard relates an incident involving the Missionaries of Charity, the religious community founded by Mother Teresa of Calcutta. Mother Teresa had accepted an invitation from the mayor of New York to convert two abandoned buildings in New York into a homeless shelter. The city agreed to "sell" the properties to the sisters for a dollar each, and developed a plan for reconstruction to provide a facility that could take care of sixty-four homeless men. Each facility would include a dining room, kitchen, and dormitory rooms. But before construction could begin, the sisters had to meet with a large number of bureaucratic officials in order to have their plan approved. After an initial approval by the appropriate department (a year and a half later) the sisters believed that their dream could be realized—until they were told that New York's building code required the installation of an elevator in every new or renovated building. The Missionaries of Charity then attempted to explain that because of their religious beliefs and practices they would never use the elevator and that the enormous cost ($100,000) would tremendously escalate their expenses. The sisters were informed that the law could not be waived. "Mother Teresa gave up. She didn't want to devote that much extra money to something that really wouldn't help the poor."[3]

Howard would argue that law in the form of unnecessary government regulation and bureaucracy is touching every aspect of our lives: "fixing the pothole in front of the house, running public schools, regulating day care centers, controlling behavior in the work place, cleaning up the environment, and deciding whether Mother Teresa gets a building permit."[4]

What is particularly annoying in regards to some of the laws in these matters is the obsession with bringing precision to regulations that govern almost every aspect of our lives. Such concern for uniformity springs from a legitimate goal: providing some assurance of universal treatment for all cases and people. But is this what has in fact been created? Howard would argue that a rigorous approach toward regulation is doomed to failure, and, not by coincidence, makes almost every encounter with government an exercise in frustration.[5]

Another frequently voiced complaint against our legal system today is the proliferation of litigation by the legal establishment itself. No one would deny that a legal system is indispensable for securing rights and freedoms. And the courts would be commended by many Americans for the protection they have given to the poor and disadvantaged. But is there a downside that emerges from protection of rights at any cost, when a society contends that every right imaginable must be protected in civil court by means of litigation? Many Americans bemoan what seems to be a lack of connection between the law and religious or moral values such as prudence, civility, and trust: "The consequent breakdown in community has fed the current explosion of lawsuits, which in turn has accelerated the breakdown of community."[6]

As Americans look at their civil courts, many now see a vast bureaucracy, entering into almost very sphere of their lives, but often very slow in administering justice. The role of the civil lawyer and of the legal system seems tarnished in the eyes of many. But what about the legal systems employed by religious institutions? The Roman Catholic Church, for example, has for centuries utilized its own procedures of law, greatly influenced by ancient Roman law and in turn has greatly influenced successor legal systems such as common law. Can any of the charges made against civil law be attributed to Church (canon) law as well? Moreover, should *any* legal system find a comfortable home in a church supposedly birthed by the Spirit and commissioned to proclaim the values of a kingdom yet to come?

This volume is a modest effort in the continuing dialogue within the contemporary Church about subscribing to a legal system. It is no secret that many members of the Church (clergy as well as laity) find no useful purpose for canon law, viewing it as arbitrary and antiquated, a relic from the past which acts as a hindrance or obstacle to the movement of the Spirit. I do not subscribe to this view although I understand how it has developed. Rather, in this book I will offer what I believe are some modern contributions to an analysis of the canonical tradition of the Church, a tradition which I believe can still serve a useful purpose in the life of the Church. There is not only a desire but a necessity to utilize law in the Church today—a situation which can be highly constructive when the law is viewed as a ministry of service.

The audience of this text is not primarily academicians, theoreticians or specialists in civil or canon law, although it is hoped that some of the reflections offered here will contribute to their dialogue on the problems that face civil and canonical professionals and on the jaded contemporary perception of their craft. The work is particularly addressed to the beleaguered pastoral ministers who struggle to proclaim the life-giving message of Jesus Christ to communities filled with many battered and broken people who bump, bruise, and hassle one another but who also seek to know Jesus' compassion and care. I believe that canon law, by providing some organization and a road map through some of its processes, can help to prevent some unnecessary aggravation and confusion in the ecclesial household.

This work is not, therefore, an introduction to canon law, in the sense of a text or treatise on individual canons or sections of the code.[7] Moreover, it will focus solely on the Latin code, and not include reference to the Eastern code,[8] which would be far beyond its scope. Its aim is much more modest. It will attempt, as a general initiation, to look briefly at some of the canonical institutions of canon law, such as the diocesan synod, the marriage tribunal, and conciliation processes, in an effort to show the relevance and place of a legal system in a faith community. The legal procedures of the Church, developed over many centuries, for the most part as a concrete attempt to respond to a "pastoral problem," can often lead to useful, nonarbitrary solutions that protect the rights of the various individuals involved.

The call of the Church since Vatican II has been towards communion—communion with Christ, communion among companion-pilgrims on the journey to the kingdom, and communion between local churches.[9] The concept of communion provides a structure and path in which each member's unique individuality, talent, and gifts can be respected, esteemed, and creatively developed for service. But this can only happen when the rights of individuals within the community are respected and protected.

The development of canon law has been sporadic and very much linked to other historical changes in the life of the Church. Chapter 1 will briefly summarize some of the major historical developments in the Church's legal history.

It is a canonical understanding that, among other duties, the pope serves the Church as her principal legislator. In 1983, Pope John Paul II, in fulfillment of this responsibility, promulgated a revised system of laws for Latin Rite Catholics, after several years of consultation and revised drafts by a papally sponsored commission. In fact Pope Paul VI (1963–78) has often been called the father of the revised code since much of the work of revision took place during his stewardship. The second chapter of this book will highlight the role of the chief legislator by reviewing some of the addresses given by these two popes in which they expressed some of their hopes for a revitalized appreciation for law within the Church after the Second Vatican Council. The ideas expressed by these popes significantly influenced the committees and various consultative bodies that drafted the codal legislation, who themselves, in turn, influenced the adaptation of the law to the new circumstances of the post–Vatican II Church. The sources for these papal insights are the annual addresses of the pope to the Roman Rota, one of the tribunals of the Holy See. In these speeches the popes have traditionally expounded on some specific part of the law, or on the role of law in the life of the Church.

Many see its emphasis on rights for all Church members as one of the most important contributions of the revised code of canon law, issued in 1983. The acceptance of human rights into Church legislation will be briefly explored (chapter 3) and one right newly incorporated into Church legislation with significant impact, especially for clerics—the right to privacy and confidentiality—will also be examined (chapter 4).

When mention is made of "canon law" or the "canon lawyer," what comes almost automatically to the Catholic mind is "annulment." This is probably to be expected, since the annulment process is where most Catholics come in contact with Church lawyers and Church legal procedures. Although it is often seen by many Catholics as a rather cold and intrusive proceeding, the annulment process has great potential for healing, growth, and reconciliation. Many people who come to the parish minister at this difficult time are filled with pain, confusion, and hurt, and cry out for help. The pastoral minister who approaches this situation with compassion and a basic understanding of the legal procedures that will be utilized by the marriage tribunal (court) can help facilitate an often much-needed reminder of Christ's compassionate care. These matters will be discussed in chapter 5.

This book will also take a look at an ancient but newly energized institution of the Church now being utilized by many dioceses, the diocesan synod (chapter 6). In many ways, this organism, though cumbersome and unpredictable, offers one of the best possibilities for encapsulating the insights of Vatican II, because of its inherent emphasis upon large-scale collaboration and consultation in the local church. In 1993, my own diocese, the Diocese of Rochester in upstate New York, culminated a detailed and broad-based canvassing of its entire Catholic population concerning issues of major importance to the local church by gathering delegates from its twelve counties in a large downtown convention center to chart with the bishop the fast-approaching journey into the next millennium. Like many dioceses seeking to mobilize their dwindling clergy resources and emerging lay talent, the Rochester synod seemed an especially resilient and exciting vehicle with which to launch a moment of renewal for the local church. The process used by this diocese will be presented, not necessarily as a blueprint for the design and implementation of other diocesan synods, but as one example of a canonical institution that has been dusted off and given new vitality with myriad possibilities for the contemporary Church.

Tension between the roles of the emerging layperson, now more involved in the life of the Church, and the roles of those who exercise authority within the Church has been an experience that has left many understandably unsettled. Chapter 7 will show how many dioceses have developed, with the encouragement of Church law itself, sensitive and sensible procedures for resolving conflicts that develop between members of the Church and, at times, between members and those in positions of authority in the Church.

For many pastoral ministers today, law seems the *problem,* rarely a solution. The 1983 *Code of Canon Law,* though of relatively recent publication, is nonetheless often perceived as an anachronism, antiquated and suppressive, assembled by elderly men, working in some murky recesses of the Vatican, for a culture and times far distant from current reality.

Thus serious questions arise. Do a code of canon law and a legal system—sometimes seen in former times as too pervasive and too powerful—have any place in the vision of the Second Vatican Council which is seen to be too "pastoral" and "spiritual"? If the Gospel is freeing and if laws are external rules that demand external conformity, are laws out of order in a life formed by the Gospel?

Three things are certain. Whereas the code of 1917 was largely unknown to most Catholic laypeople, since it was a work designed primarily for the professional canonist, the code of canon law recently issued—if it is to have significant impact upon the life of all of the people of God—must be seen to have a different purpose than its predecessor.

Second, canon law must never be seen as an end in itself. "[C]anon law is meant to preserve, protect and encourage all those common undertakings designed to make us more faithful and more persevering in the practice of Christian living. It does this by devoting the first place to the Spirit, which is the supreme law."[10]

Third, canon law will seem superfluous if it does not respect the ability of mature people to make responsible decisions as they attempt to respond in their own lives to the call of Christ to live each day the Gospel message. Officeholders in the Church will need to develop a new way of thinking about the use of law in the Church, a way true to the conciliar vision which saw all authority as service to the community. The primary self-understanding of the Church continues to be evangelical, not juridical: "[T]he gospel is the good news of God's freeing, loving, unifying, dignifying act for all people. Any just statement of the place of law must set the law within a great inbreaking of divine compassion."[11]

Canon law will never be able to define completely the Church and its mission, which the Second Vatican Council in the constitution *Lumen Gentium* described as "mystery."[12] Yet it will always be necessary that any community, even a Christian community, have some characteristic body or structure and some explicit regulations.

The role of law in the Church is better clarified today as its relationship to theology is explored. Ladislaus Örsy has been instrumental in developing this theme. The role of theology is to provide the community with *values,* an overall vision, and self-definition, while canon law is asked to provide norms for action, for the appropriation of those values which are meant to serve the community. "Thus the two worlds meet. If they join and work together in harmony, there is a wholeness, a true integrity of life in the community from which peace follows. If they do not work in harmony, the community is divided 'in its spirit'; there is a split between what it sees and what it does."[13] Each and every value that the Church promotes must be permeated by its God-given "supernatural" purpose. Or as canon 1752 puts it, "the salvation of souls . . . must always be the supreme law."

In the last few years, one of the expressions that has become popular in describing an effective approach to Church ministry is the claim that it must be *pastoral.* But, as Örsy says, it may perhaps be better to say that the law, all laws in the Church, must have a *redeeming* quality; that is, the Church must have a legal system that speaks emphatically of herself as the servant Church that is faithful to its servant-leader and founder, Jesus.[14] Law can be a valuable and redeeming tool, helping the community to achieve its common servant ideals and values as these are articulated by theology: our call to be in salvific communion with one another and with the Lord, and our call to protect individual dignity and to respect each person.

CHAPTER ONE

The Development of Law within the Church

Historically, tensions, problems, and differences of opinion are inevitable in human societies, with the consequent need for law and some sense of order so that particular societies do not break apart. Many of the principles of our legal tradition still in use today, both secular and religious, have emerged in primitive historical situations from decades and even centuries long past. The more we look at societies of the past, the more we see ourselves—and the more the legal answers to the complexities of primitive humankind continue to sustain our search for tranquillity today.

Within religious history Judaism has contributed much to our understanding of the relevance of law to a religious system, for law is central to Judaism, as that which binds member to member and member to God. As God says to Joshua:

> Only be strong and stand very firm and be careful to keep the whole Law which my servant Moses laid down for you. Do not swerve from this either to right or left, and then you will succeed wherever you go. Have the book of the Law always on your lips; meditate on it day and night, so that you may carefully keep everything that is written in it. Then your undertakings will prosper, then you will have success. (Josh. 1:6–8)[1]

Observance of the law was a faithful response of the community to the God who rescued Israel from slavery when she was a poor and oppressed people in Egypt. The prophets of the tradition would later remind Israel of her relationship to God in the law and the various legal prescriptions, and of her need to return to a life of justice.

The Christian Scriptures, especially in the Gospel of Matthew, continue a concern for the law as part of the religious experience. Jesus in Matthew's Gospel is portrayed as the new Moses and the prophet of the new Israel:

> Do not imagine that I have come to abolish the Law or the Prophets. I have come not to abolish but to complete them. . . . Therefore, anyone who infringes even one of the least of these commandments and teaches others to do the same will be considered the least in the Kingdom of Heaven; but the person who keeps them and teaches them will be considered great in the Kingdom of Heaven. (Matt. 5:17, 19)

Jesus is the uncompromising teacher and interpreter of the law of the kingdom and Matthew presents the law—the commandments of Jesus—as a significant element of the Good News.[2] Law is primary in the proclamation of the Good News of redemption: "To follow Jesus means to be obedient to the commandments of Jesus. In the Gospel of Matthew, 'law' has become 'gospel.'"[3]

Jesus fulfills the law and the prophets. Obeying the laws of God and keeping God's commandments resulted in blessings for the people of Israel. "By living in accordance with the law, the Israelites entered into and experienced the true meaning and nature of life. . . . Obedience to the law brought with it the experience of the good life."[4] The law, the "Torah," had been the great blessing, the essence of all that was good and holy for the Israelites. In their obedience to the commandments, the Israelites discover that they are the "People of God."

Now, in Matthew, admission to the new community of Israel established by Jesus is not based on birth but on obedience to the *new* Torah—the commandments of Jesus. The Church's ongoing mission of teaching the new law, the commandments of Jesus, is rooted in Jesus' presence within the community. Jesus calls forth a new community and presents it with a new law for the realization of life.

The Jew could pray with exaltation Psalm 119: "How I love your law! I ponder it all day long. . . . I am wiser than all my teachers, because I ponder your instructions." For Christians inspired by Matthew's depiction of the new Moses, the great law of love will direct them to fullness of life.

The complexities of life in the early Church demanded a somewhat more complicated legal system than the scriptural expressions could supply, though the premises of the Church's legal instruction would remain based on scriptural warrant. But before developing their own legal structures, Christians had first to determine the approach to the law imposed on them by virtue of Roman citizenship. One of the first developments of Christian jurisprudence, established by actual historical experience, was the principle of civil disobedience: laws that conflict with Christian faith and tradition cannot bind the conscience and may be disobeyed. Precedents in the Jewish tradition were numerous: resistance to Baal worship and the righteous disobedience of Daniel to King Darius, for example. When challenged by any conquering nation, Israel had to remain faithful to its laws. However, as Berman indicates, when Christians defied the laws of the Romans, they were defying the laws of many of their own people.[5] Thus a principle of Christian legal jurisprudence is the assertion of a moral right to violate a law that is in conflict with God's law. A positive impact upon the Roman law by the Church can also be observed. Examples cited can include: giving the wife a position of equality before the law, requiring mutual consent of both spouses for the validity of a marriage, and abolishing the power of the father over the life or death of his children.[6]

It may be helpful now to list briefly some of the particular highlights in the historical development of law in the Church through the centuries. Very significant for the history of canon law is the sixth century, which saw the beginning of collections of law which were chronologically arranged. These collections included not only the canons of the great councils of the East but also decretals, official letters of the popes, usually in the form of responses to inquiries from various bishops, all of which gradually gained considerable weight as legislative sources. The first great compiler of such a collection (and the first great Western canonist known to us by name) was Dionysius Exiguus (or Denis the Little), a monk from southwestern Russia who had been summoned by Pope Gelasius to Rome at the close of the fifth century to organize the papal archives and to compile a collection of legal texts.[7] Systematization of laws into collections was regarded as an important legal necessity, indicative of the belief that the law, if it was to be useful, had to be organized in some way in order to be accessible.

The collection assembled by Dionysius became appropriately known as the *Dionysiana,* and because of its organization and systematization, was widely copied and distributed. Some of the issues addressed by this collection included "familiar crimes running the gamut from abortion to nepotism, and some less familiar ones such as necromancy and the celebration of birthdays during lent."[8] The *Dionysiana* was to become the nucleus for most Western collections of law in the Church for the next six hundred years.

These collections were made up of "canons" (coming from the Greek for "rule") and included norms for every facet of the religious life of the people. Included in their purview were forms for ceremonies and the celebration of the sacraments, regulations governing when various liturgical celebrations took place (the liturgical calendar), and norms concerning distribution of alms to the poor and the powers and qualifications of officeholders in the Church.[9] One additional area of life that saw much regulation was that of marriage and the family.

Another monk whose name is reverenced by canonists is Gratian, a professor at the University of Bologna in the twelfth century. Not much is known about Gratian beyond his monastic status and professorship at Bologna. But he was to define significantly the course of canon law for succeeding centuries. As the Church became more defensive against an increasingly hostile and secularized environment in Europe which challenged the Church's authority, an updated and further systematized collection of law was urgently needed. From a variety of collections, Gratian used miscellaneous scattered decisions and decrees that had been pronounced by various popes, councils, and bishops and assembled the legal texts into an orderly system of jurisprudence. Using the dialectical methodology of the theologian Abelard, he was able to assemble his *Concordance of Discordant Canons* (also called the *Decretum*), which became *the* resource for all those involved in canon law. But, as might be expected, Gratian's work illustrated a critical flaw in canon law: without any clear method of appending newer laws to previous collections, the

Decretum quickly became outdated. By the early part of the thirteenth century, Pope Gregory IX (c. 1170–1241) sensed this problem and invited Raymond of Penyafort (c. 1180–1275), a noted Spanish canonist, to assemble a new collection of decretal law to include papal decrees issued since Gratian's collection. *The Decretals of Gregory IX* received Gregory's official seal of approval, thereby making it the first official collection of laws promulgated for use in the entire Church. This compilation continued in use until the close of the thirteenth century. Then a new collection was prepared under Boniface VIII (c. 1235–1303), called the "Sixth Book" because it was an addition to the five books that made up the great Gratian *Decretum*.

Canonical development up to the sixteenth century was summarized in the publication of the *Corpus Iuris Canonici* (Body of Canon Law) that included Gratian's *Decretum*, the decretals of Gregory IX and Boniface VIII, and subsequent collections of decretals. Arranged by John Chappuis and Vitale de Thebis in 1500, it became, along with the decrees of the Council of Trent, the main reference for canonical norms until the first code of canon law was issued in 1917.

As part of his program for renewing the life of the Church and in response to requests by bishops for a systematized collection of laws that had been made since the premature closing of the First Vatican Council, Pope Pius X, elected to the papacy in 1903, appointed Cardinal Pietro Gasparri to undertake responsibility for a new venture in canon law. The fruit of Gasparri's arduous task was a code, resembling the Napoleonic codes quite common in Europe, with all the appropriate canons now arranged in one book under five topics. This code, published in 1917, marks a milestone in the history of canon law. Now, for the first time, the Church's laws were organized into one comprehensive source for easy reference (for those who understood Latin!). The new code was a great success. "It was handy, well-ordered and accessible (just 2,414 canons) and canonists took to it with relish."[10] Even though it may seem to readers that a code of canon law had been in use for centuries, it was actually only at the beginning of the twentieth century that such a book came into being. It remained the primary tool for canonists for the next several decades.

But as newer norms were required to address the needs of the Church in a constantly changing world, Pope John XXIII, even as he announced his momentous decision in 1959 to convene an ecumenical council, also called for a revision of the 1917 code. After John's death in 1963, Pope Paul VI completed the work of Vatican II and strove to implement its various documents and decrees. Paul's papacy was thus a time for interim law-making, laws which would eventually be incorporated into a new code. Paul VI greatly influenced the new code, although he did not live to see its completion. He gave many speeches in which he shared his hopes for a new approach to law—a new *habitus mentis*, or new perspective—that would make law a more vibrant and pastoral tool in the Church.

Pope John Paul II, elected to the papacy in October 1978, brought to fruition a labor of several years, promulgating in 1983 the new *Code of Canon Law*. He saw this volume as, in a certain sense, an effort to translate the conciliar doctrine and ecclesiology of Vatican II into "canonical language."[11] Seven years later, this revision was completed by the issuance of a code for the Eastern Churches, thereby fulfilling the dream of Pope John XXIII for an updated legislative system for the entire Catholic Church.

CHAPTER TWO

The Mind of the Legislator

IN THE LEGISLATIVE TRADITION OF THE CHURCH, THE "MIND of the legislator" has always had an important role. Most canons in the code of canon law are "ecclesiastical law" (human laws, enactments of the Church's own authority and therefore alterable, as opposed to "divine law," drawn directly from God's revelation). They therefore need, as do all human laws, interpretation in accordance with certain prescribed principles. Canon 17, for example, includes in its list of procedures for interpretation reference to the "mind of the legislator," based on the principle that the legislator should know the meaning of the law he has promulgated.[1]

But in addition, the mind of the legislator should be studied to ascertain his approach to the meaning and place of law in the Church. For this reason, it is appropriate to review some of the addresses made by two recent popes to the Roman Rota that have in some ways influenced the universal legislation now in effect.

The Roman Rota is a church tribunal in Rome which deals primarily with marriage cases that have been appealed to Rome for a final determination.[2] Each year for the past several decades, beginning with Pope Pius XII, the popes have given a major address to the Rota, inaugurating the judicial year. Quite frequently in these speeches, the popes have discussed some point of law or comment on the role of law in ecclesial life.

Paul VI

In 1963 Pope Paul VI used the occasion of his Rotal address to discuss his vision of law and the role of the canon lawyer in the

Church. Paul saw the providing of justice as an important service of canonical ministry and he believed that canonical procedures deserved careful study on the part of the judges, especially when their decisions affected the consciences of people.[3]

Another important concern, articulated frequently in the addresses of both Paul VI and John Paul II, has been the role of law in the protection of human rights. Paul forcefully reminded the auditors (judges) of the Rota that new emphases were needed in the revised law:

> Who is not aware that the domain of human rights is being constantly extended as human dignity becomes ever clearer? This extension of rights must also be taken into account in the new Code of Canon Law whose revision cannot be simply an amending of the previous Code by the introduction [of] . . . a more appropriate order of material, the addition of what seems worthwhile, and the omission of no longer relevant material. Rather, the Code must become an instrument adapted for Church life in the post-Vatican II era.[4]

Relationship of Canon Law and the Second Vatican Council

The relationship of the forthcoming code to the Vatican Council was also consistently emphasized in Paul's addresses, since there had to be a connection between the theological developments of the council and the laws which would implement them, through applying to the juridical life of the Church the general principles set down by the council. Paul closely linked theology with law:

> Thus, the new Code will avoid the danger of a disastrous separation between Spirit and institution, and between theology and law, for law and pastoral authority will be understood theologically as a means of spreading the peace of Christ, which is the work of divine—not human—justice.[5]

Paul claimed that justice will be promoted and preserved in the new code by fostering the participation of all members of the Church, cleric and lay, since the faithful "are not to be regarded as subjects only, but also as co-workers with the hierarchy, to which at every level, they render respectful support."[6]

Justice will also be protected, in the view of Paul, by a careful and thoughtful emphasis on the proper role of law, not by unnecessarily expanding or exaggerating its role—a danger that had manifested itself too often in the past: "It [justice] will appear rather as one facet of . . . life—truly an important one—but also one serving the life of the communion as such and leaving to the individual believer the freedom and responsibility . . . needed to build up the body of Christ."[7] Paul hoped to dispel the popular misconception that somehow the Second Vatican Council had eliminated the need for canon law in the Church. Law, he believed, would always be needed to assist in the orderly carrying out of the gospel demands, and to protect the true freedom of the individual Church member. "How true it is," Paul reflected, "that a human without law is no longer human! How true it is in practice that a law without an authority to teach, interpret, and enjoin easily becomes obscure, annoys and vanishes."[8]

Time and again, in these allocutions, Paul returns to the theme of the relation of canon law to the theological developments of the Second Vatican Council, and, as a corollary, the integration of canon law with pastoral perspectives: "As canon law after the Council must bear the imprint of the pastoral character in its foundation, interpretation and application, it seems . . . that it must impress upon the law of the Church a more human quality, and where there is a necessity, a greater sensitivity to charity. It is charity that the law must promote and protect in the ecclesial community and with respect to secular society."[9] He reminded the Church of the true nature of pastoral authority: "It [the law] must be conscious of the nature of ecclesial authority—a service, a ministry, a work of love. It must direct its attention more explicitly to the defense of the human person and the formation of the Christian for communitarian participation in Catholic life."[10]

Subsidiarity

Paul also encouraged the implementation of subsidiarity, the principle that the higher authority or structure should intervene only when the common good requires it and that suitable discretionary latitude should be granted to pastors and others. The laws then promulgated should be infused with spiritual dynamics: "The laws of the code should breathe the spirit of charity and restraint, kindness and moderation, which must distinguish the new code from every purely human legislation."[11] Such a perspective will require, in Paul's view, a new way of looking at the use of power and authority in the Church. Any hint of arbitrariness in the legal system must be avoided. Authority must be viewed only as service, and those who hold office in the Church must constantly look to the good of those for whose sake their authority is exercised. Paul quoted St. Bernard of Clairvaux to Pope Eugene III: "We must be fully aware that we have been given a ministry, not ownership."[12]

The Gospel, far from abolishing authority, institutes and establishes it, placing it in the service of others. Jesus wanted his community to be structured and joined in unity and to be, however, not only a hierarchical structure but also a spiritual and visible social organism. Since she is also a social reality, the Church will require visible structures and external norms. But Paul's constant refrain in these allocutions was that canon law must devote first place to the spirit which is its supreme law.

The Pastoral Character of Law

Paul claimed that good law in the Church is always pastoral by its very nature. Its influence is felt in the sphere of the human side of the Church, in its existence as a human as well as a divine society.

One of the differences in the Church's legal posture, as distinct from that of the secular law, is the emphasis that should be given to equity: justice tempered with the sweetness of mercy. Paul claimed that "if societal life requires the determination of human law, nevertheless the norms of this law, inevitably general and abstract, cannot foresee the concrete circumstances in which the laws will be later applied."[13] It was Paul's hope that the spirit of law embodied in such principles as canonical *equity* would imbue the ecclesiastical judge with moderation and mercy in his/her ministry: "[The judge] will take account of the human person and of the demands of a given

situation, which may compel the judge to apply the law more se-
verely, but ordinarily they will lead [the judge] to exercise it in a
more human and compassionate manner."[14] Such an approach to law
should infuse juridical procedures as well: "You want the justice,
which you must exercise with canonical equity, to be speedier; more
gentle; more even-tempered."[15]

At times, Paul admitted, the Church and its law have been
negatively influenced by the secular society in which it has found
itself and has taken upon itself some of its negative features: "It is
unfortunately true that the Church, in the exercise of her power,
whether judicial (procedural) or coercive (penal) has in the course of
the centuries borrowed from civil legislation certain serious imper-
fections, even methods which were unjust in the true and proper
sense, at least objectively speaking."[16]

What, according to Paul, needed attention among those who exercise a ministry of law was a new pastoral *style* that would be in conformity with the vision of the council: "The law is not for the law's
sake, nor judgment for the judgment's sake, but both law and judgment are at the service of truth, justice, patience and charity—
virtues which constitute today more than ever what should stamp the
character of the ecclesiastical judge."[17] The virtues which should
characterize the church official are, he said, *love* and *humanity*. "What
shines forth most in your mission is precisely *Christian charity*, which
adds greater dignity and greater fruitfulness to the *equity* (aequitas)
of judgments that was the source of so much honor for Roman
law."[18] The judge must interiorize the values which the law wishes
to dispense in its ministry: "[The judge] needs a complete moral
uprightness—one would try in vain to create it, if the judge lacks it
in the first place."[19] He then went on to outline in detail the specific
qualities of a good servant of justice (these are, in fact, also applicable
to any representative of a modern legal judiciary):

> You need impartiality . . . and that presupposes a profound
> and unshakable honesty. You need disinterestedness, because
> there is a danger that courts can be under pressure from ex-
> traneous interests—greed, politics, favoritism and so on. You
> need concern, so that you will take the cause of justice to heart
> because you are aware that it is a lofty service for him who

is just and merciful, and righteous (Ps. 112[111]:4, "righteous judge" (2 Tim 4:8), "faithful and just" (1 John 1:9).[20]

Pope Paul VI saw new and expanded possibilities for law in service to the Church after the Second Vatican council. And just as the council would dramatically change the contours of theological speculation, so too, a "new way of doing business" would characterize all practitioners of Church law, one requiring a wholly new theologically informed legal mentality.

John Paul II

Karol Wojtyla began his ministry as pastor of the universal Church in October 1978. Like the popes who preceded him, he also gave annual addresses to the Roman Rota at the inauguration of the judicial year. In many of his addresses, John Paul II gave attention to the legal procedures and principles of law that he believed needed renewed emphasis, particularly if he thought that some aspect of the law needed improvement, or needed to be better observed. But he also spoke about the function of law in the Church, since he saw it as having an important role in safeguarding rights, particularly human rights, a cause near to his heart.

Law as Defender of the Human Person

The Church, John Paul II believed, had a duty in a world that is often characterized by injustice and violence to be a strong defender of the human person:

> As the Church's self-awareness has developed, the human-Christian person has found not only recognition but also, and above all, an explicit, active and balanced defense of personal basic rights in harmony with those of the ecclesial community. This, too, is a duty the Church cannot renounce.[21]

Canon law can help the wider community by teaching what it means to be truly human in today's world. Canon law will accomplish this lofty goal by its affirmation of the self "as an authentically social being through acknowledgement of and respect for the other as a person endowed with universal, inviolable, and inalienable rights and invested with a transcendent dignity."[22]

Respect for the dignity of the human person is, in John Paul's view, at the core of proper protection of human rights. The law provides protection by its use of administrative procedures and judicial processes that enhance the dignity of the human person. The Church must protect the rights of the individual person, but it must likewise promote and protect the common good, which may even at times require the imposition of penalties, one of the more onerous aspects of ecclesiastical law. Penalties—such as excommunication—are still needed, according to John Paul, so that the rights of *all* members—the legacy of the common good—are protected.

Pastoral Quality of Law

John Paul continued the theme of his predecessor, Paul VI, in stressing the pastoral quality and nature of canon law in the modern Church. In his allocution "Pastoral Nature of Canon Law and Respect for Truth,"[23] he reminded the Rota that the conciliar spirit of Vatican II emphasized the legitimate purposes of law, including the *pastoral*:

> The pastoral nature of this law, that is, its function within the salvific mission of the pastors of the Church and the entire People of God, thus finds a solid basis in conciliar ecclesiology according to which the visible aspects of the Church are linked inseparably to the invisible ones—forming a single unified whole—comparable to the mystery of the Incarnate Word (*Lumen Gentium,* no. 8). On the other hand, the Council did not fail to draw many practical consequences from this pastoral character of canon law, by taking concrete measures to ensure that canonical laws and structures might always be more suited to the welfare of souls (cf. *Christus Dominus,* passim).[24]

John Paul II expanded upon Paul VI's references to "canonical equity" and other legal concepts which grant exceptions to the law, usually on the basis of the extenuating circumstances of the individual that could not have been foreseen by the law.

> The law is not only human when it grants exceptions but should be seen as fully pastoral in scope. This is based on the fact that justice and law in the strict sense—and consequently general norms, proceedings, sanctions, and other typical expressions should they become necessary—are required in the Church for the good of souls and are therefore intrinsically pastoral.[25]

There was therefore, in John Paul's mind, a close association between the Church's legal system and its pastoral vision since they have a common goal: the salvation of souls. But there is more. Pastoral work always includes a dimension of justice. In fact, it will be impossible, he said, to lead souls toward the kingdom of heaven without the minimum of love and prudence that is found in the commitment to seeing that the law and the rights of all in the Church are observed faithfully.[26]

On another occasion after attending an ecumenical prayer meeting with various religious leaders in Assisi, John Paul reflected on the role of canon law in strengthening and restoring peace to ecclesial society. He quoted the distinguished jurist Francesco Carnelutti, who declared: "People above all need to live in peace. Justice is the condition for peace. . . . People reach this state of mind when there is order in and around them. Justice is conformity to the order of the universe. Law is just when it really serves to put order into society" (F. Carnelutti, *Come nasce il diritto,* 1954, p. 53).[27] Those involved in the ministry of law must foster this peace by their involvement in the search for truth, a voyage that is not always easy. "[I]ts [truth's] affirmation is sometimes quite demanding. Nevertheless, it must always be respected in human communication and human relations."[28]

In the mind of both Paul VI and John Paul II, law continues to have many redeeming roles in the contemporary Church. It must help to maintain the *communio* of all the Churches. It must be vigilant in protecting human rights and making sure that there are available venues for recourse when someone feels aggrieved that his/her proper rights have been violated or compromised. The Church in its legal system must mirror justice, showing itself to the world as a society living the values of justice which its founder sought to preach and teach. The Church must also make sure that its officials and administrators work assiduously to promote in their own judicial activity the values of the law. Finally, those who administer justice in the Church should refrain from a rigorous, unbending approach to law when mercy and compassion which are, in fact, encouraged by the law should prevail.

innate dignity that raises him/her above all creation. The dignity of the human person must consequently be the measure of all just economic activity.

c. Since the human being is sacred, the individual possesses God-granted rights which are not conferred by society nor dependent on the good will of the state, but are inherent and inalienable.

d. Rights do not exist apart from duties, but rather are correlative with duties. Each right also implies a corresponding duty to recognize rights in others.

The Canonical Implementation of Basic Rights

The 1983 *Code of Canon Law* goes much further than previous universal Church legislation in recognizing basic rights. Canon 87 of the 1917 code had stated simply that baptism constitutes a human being as a person in the Church with all the rights and duties of Christians,[10] without much elaboration or specification as to those rights and duties.

A significant contribution of the 1983 code was its recognition in law of several rights, including some specific human rights, for all the Christian faithful.[11] One of the major influences for the inclusion and clarification of rights, including human rights, in the revised code was the development of the "principles for revision" approved by the first synod of bishops in 1967. They were to serve as an important set of references for revision of the code.

In April 1967, a central committee of consultors from the Pontifical Commission for the Revision of the Code of Canon Law, under the direction of Cardinal Pericle Felici, the second president of the commission (1966–82), set out to develop several fundamental principles to aid in the task of revision. The principles they developed attempted to guarantee a certain harmony and consistency in all the later drafts of the revised law for the new code. It is encouraging to note how many of these principles concerned the development and protection of rights. For example, the first principle, after identifying the fact that the new code must be juridic in character to be usable as a legislative document, indicated that the essential object of canon law is the determination and safeguarding of the rights and obligations of each person.[12] The sixth principle established that the revised code is to acknowledge, define, and articulate rights which persons possess by natural law, by divine positive law, and by their proper juridical condition in the Church.[13] The seventh principle stated the need for implementing structures which would safeguard subjective rights: "Nor is it enough to say that the safeguarding of human rights is adequately provided for in our legislation. We must also acknowledge the truly personal subjective rights, without which a juridically organized society cannot be imagined."[14]

According to the "principles for revision," the sensitivity for rights must extend to all in the Church: "In Canon Law, we must, therefore, proclaim that the principle of the juridical protection of rights applies with equal measure to superiors and subjects alike, so that any suspicion whatsoever of arbitrariness in church administration may completely disappear."[15] To remove the dangers of arbitrariness in the exercise of authority and to protect proper rights more effectively, a revised system of recourse (in which actions or lack of appropriate action by someone in authority could be appealed to a higher authority) was recommended:

> Although it is generally thought that recourses and judicial appeals are sufficiently provided for in the Code of Canon Law [1917] according to the demands of justice, it is nevertheless the common opinion of canonists that administrative recourses are still lacking considerably in church practice and in the administration of justice. Hence the need is everywhere strongly felt to set up in the Church administrative tribunals of various degrees and kinds, so that defense of one's rights can be taken up in these tribunals according to proper canonical procedures before authorized officials of different ranks.[16]

In the pursuit of justice, the principles stated that these procedures should be as open as possible, that the individual's rights might be clearly identified and protected: "It is however necessary that in any procedure, whether judicial or administrative, the one who has lodged a recourse or has been accused must be informed of all the charges made against him."[17]

The Pontifical Commission of the Code, as reaffirmed by the synod of bishops, had thus established the protection of rights as one of the bases for the revision of universal Church legislation, in principles that insisted that power not be used arbitrarily and that the rights of each member of the Church be acknowledged and protected.

Human Rights Canonically Recognized

The canonist and civil attorney James Coriden has argued forcefully that human rights which now appear in the code should be considered "constitutional," or of primary essence and significance in the Church, even though the Church has no written "constitution" as such. He argues from six points:[18]

1. The rights had their origin in a document that was intended to be "constitutional," the *Lex Ecclesiae Fundamentalis*.[19]
2. These rights are uniquely mandated by the "principles for revision" for the code.
3. The Apostolic Constitution *Sacrae Disciplinae Leges* of Pope John Paul II which promulgated the *Code of Canon Law* asserts that rights are a chief purpose of the code.[20]
4. These rights are situated in one of the books appearing early in the code, "The People of God," thereby accentuating their importance, since they are included in that section where membership within the community and its characteristics are delineated.
5. The content of the rights is of basic importance; they are fundamental claims.
6. John Paul II, the chief legislator, singled out the charter of rights for special attention just after the promulgation of the code.

According to Coriden, such a "constitutional status" gives these rights a priority. Hence, when a person in authority is considering a course of action that may have significant impact upon the freedom of others, his first concern must be whether rights will be endangered by his intended action.

The Council Fathers had a vision of the Church where rights would be esteemed and acknowledged, and it is now recognized by the *Code of Canon Law* (1983) that Catholics have the right:

a. to let their pastors know of their spiritual needs and how they should be fulfilled (canon 213);
b. to advise church leaders about what is good for the Church (canon 212 §3);
c. to form associations of like-minded people and to work for programs consistent with the teachings of the Church (canon 225 §1);
d. to enjoy a good name and reputation (canon 220);
e. to enjoy academic freedom (canon 218);
f. to perform certain roles in the liturgy (canon 835 §4);
g. to help oversee Church finances (canon 537);
h. to receive a fair trial and protection from illegally imposed sanctions (canon 221);
i. to be free of coercion in choosing a state of life (canon 219).

Not all the rights are of the same origin, nor are they of the same level. Some are basic, fundamental, human rights (which every Christian enjoys as a human being, whether the right is in the code or not), and some are more specifically Christian ones. Since human rights have been thus incorporated into the code of 1983, they can now be seen as a proper subject for ecclesial law. As one canonist has commented: "We do not lose our humanity when we are baptized: if grace builds on nature then the rights which arise from human nature remain ours as Christians."[21]

Moreover, some efforts have also been made towards concretizing the works of justice in the code itself. The lives of clerics and religious men and women as well as all of the Christian faithful, should reflect the call to social consciousness and awareness: for example, making sure that ministers and employees are given just remuneration for their services (canons 231 §2 and 1286). Social justice in the Church is also evident in the obligation, imposed especially on clerics and religious, not to tolerate sexism or racism within the Christian community. In addition, pastors are required to be attentive to social justice issues since justice is so clearly a part of the Gospel they are called to preach:

> Issues of social justice, an important part of that gospel, must therefore be included within this teaching activity. Further, since priests in their ministry "above all are the place where the Church and the world come into contact," attention to social justice concerns must be a part of the service which they give to the parish community. In this regard, pastors are to promote the apostolic role of the faithful vis-à-vis these concerns.[22]

The message of the Gospel is the dignity of the individual. The role of canon law in affirming human rights is therefore a significant one, even while it leaves to theology the task of discerning the particular social teachings which are appropriate and necessary to a particular time—for example, today's theological needs which include teachings pertinent to respect for life, the wide disparity between the rich and poor, the use of nuclear weapons, and so forth. As the basis for its pronouncements, the Church looks to the Gospel of Jesus Christ and the centrality of the dignity of the human person.

The Church will be judged concerning human rights by its own practice. Its prophetic defense of human rights and of the dignity of the human person can be credible only if the Church itself is perceived by others to be just. Its service to human rights thus pledges the Church to a constant examination of conscience and to a continuous purification and renewal of its own life, laws, institutions, and conduct.[23]

The Church's commitment to human rights, it is hoped, will be its crowning jewel: "The Church's commitment to the foundation, interpretation, and defense of human dignity and human rights is gauged not just by its words; but far more by its action and life. Least of all by the Church must the thirst for justice and the yearning for humanity be disappointed."[24]

CHAPTER FOUR

Select Church Issues in Confidentiality: Screening Procedures, Personnel Files

MANY DIFFICULTIES CONCERNING CONFIDENTIALITY FACE administrators in today's Church. In the not too distant past, great secrecy shrouded any aspect of the Church that showed it or its ministers in a bad light. But such silence is now quickly labeled by the public and the media as a "cover-up." The pendulum has now swung to such an extent that the Church is seeking to be as open as possible and "up-front" in dealing with its various public constituencies.

Such openness has become a particularly urgent question in areas such as personnel records. The last few years have seen an explosion in the number of records that are now maintained for personnel who are employed in and by the Church. Every ordained minister serving in the Church has a "personnel file," a personal dossier containing, among many possible documents, sacramental record information (sacraments that have been received), seminary and scholastic information, various reports, evaluations, complaint letters, psychological screening reports, etc., all maintained by his bishop or by his superior (if the priest is a member of a religious community).

Bishops have entrusted to certain delegates responsibility for planning personnel placement while reserving to themselves, as bishops, their canonical responsibility to actually make the appointments of clerics in the diocese. Many dioceses have instituted personnel boards whereby priests, generally elected from the ranks of the local presbyterate, assist the director (or delegate or vicar) for priest personnel in planning the placement of local clergy.

Such procedures for placement have been hailed as an effort to involve clerics in the selection of their own assignments and as a way of involving the presbyterate in more concrete consultation. But at the same time there has been some concern expressed about the confidentiality of records that are to be maintained by the diocesan bishop. There is at least the potential risk that certain matters of a confidential nature, including psychological records and reports which have been addressed to clerics within the diocese, will through the mechanism of personnel boards be more accessible to a greater number of individuals than should have access to these materials.

At the same time, many diocesan bishops in recent times have found themselves faced with litigation brought in secular courts by victims of alleged improprieties by members of the clergy. When clerics engage in behavior which brings damage to a member of the Church it is a terrible violation of trust. However, when allegations have been made and suspicions have been raised about a particular cleric and before any determination has been made concerning his innocence or guilt, it is essential that certain human rights, especially the right to a good name and to a good reputation, be respected. Civil courts have pressed, often successfully, for the right of access to clergy personnel records. However, in attempting to respond in a correct and lawful manner to these demands, certain canonical responsibilities must be observed by dioceses to protect the confidentiality of personnel records.

In a related issue, it has become increasingly more common for clerics to utilize the services of psychological resource personnel such as psychiatrists, psychologists, and social workers, as they struggle with the complex demands of service in the contemporary Church. Such opportunities for professional help for clerics are sought not only by concerned bishops but often times, and courageously, by the clerics themselves. Who, besides the bishop, may properly have access to the written records and evaluations which frequently emerge from these consultations, and what safeguards to protect the confidentiality of these records ought to be maintained?

The issues of privacy and confidentiality, as well as of public disclosure, are relevant to the written records in the Catholic Church today in many areas of its life and ministry. The 1983 *Code of Canon Law* has attempted to deal with these matters on the basis of the principles of dignity and respect for the person.

The Development of the Church's Teaching on Privacy

The right of privacy has been identified through various encyclicals and Church teachings as a basic human right which should be protected by Church legislation. As we have seen, human rights were carefully highlighted and included in the 1983 code. The right of "confidentiality" is maintained under two aspects: the right of privacy and the right to a good reputation.

Article 26 of the Second Vatican Council's Pastoral Constitution, *Gaudium et Spes*, included many of the rights that had been stated in *Pacem in Terris*, the encyclical of Pope John XXIII, including the rights to a good name and to privacy:

> At the same time, however, there is a growing awareness of the sublime dignity of the human person, who stands above all things and whose rights and duties are universal and inviolable. He ought, therefore, to have ready access to all that is necessary for living a genuinely human life: for example, food, clothing, housing, the right freely to choose his state of life, and set up a family, the right to education, work, *to his good name*, to *respect*, to proper knowledge, the right to act according to the dictates of conscience, and to *safeguard his privacy*.[1]

Both the right to a good reputation and the right to privacy were discussed by two committees of the code commission which were both attempting to draft a list of the rights of the Christian faithful for inclusion in the yet to be promulgated revised code. One of the committees (drafting the schema on the laity) realized that any listing of rights for members of the Church should include an expressed recognition of such human rights as the right to privacy and the right to a good reputation. After much discussion and many reformulations, a canon was composed which combined the content of *Pacem in Terris* and *Gaudium et Spes*: "No one is permitted to damage unlawfully the good reputation which another person enjoys or to violate the right of another person to protect his or her own privacy" (canon 220). This canon, included in Book II of the code, is part of the section entitled "Obligations and Rights of the Christian Faithful," which includes all those baptized and incorporated into the Church. The right extends to all the baptized, whether they be clergy or laity.

Privacy and Psychological Screening Procedures

Of some considerable help in framing the right of privacy has been the protection historically afforded to vowed religious in their relationship to religious superiors. Canon 630 of the 1983 code (reaffirming canon 530 of the 1917 code) protects religious in their right to privacy by forbidding their superiors to force or induce them to manifest their consciences about extremely sensitive and personal matters. For several years now, religious communities have struggled with the question of the possible violation of this privacy by the use of psychological testing. Modern psychological techniques that provide diagnostic evaluations of religious have been called into question by the implicit possibility of creating an environment where such a manifestation of conscience may inadvertently take place, since many of these tests utilize stimuli that are purposely structured—even if ambiguously—to uncover concealed attitudes.

It could, therefore, be an abuse of the right of privacy for a superior to instruct a member to undergo testing that would result in a report containing material within the realm of conscience. Yet the need for psychological screening of candidates for religious life has been expressed even by the Holy See. The "General Statutes" annexed to the Apostolic Constitution *Sedes Sapientiae*, in discussing the admission of candidates to the novitiate, state the need for both a physical and a psychological assessment.[2]

Moreover, Pope Pius XII, in an address to a congress of the International Association of Applied Psychology on April 10, 1958, discussed the inviolable right of the person to keep secret the content of his/her psyche. There exists, explained the pope, an area of the inner psyche which deserves most careful consideration by therapeutic counselors, an area of "tendencies and dispositions . . . so hidden that the individual will never know its existence."[3] Pius XII gave strong warning to those who would violate the inner dimensions of the human psyche. "And just as it is illicit to appropriate another's goods or to make an attempt on his bodily integrity without his consent, so it is not permissible to enter into his inner domain against his will, whatever the technique or method used."[4]

The instruction of the Sacred Congregation for Religious, *Renovationis Causam* (January 6, 1969), expressed support for psychological assessments in vocational screening. But it also cautioned that their use be restricted to exceptional cases in the selection of candidates. The document further underscored that such screening by a qualified psychologist should be performed with a fully consenting candidate who has given permission for such a test. The principles of *informed consent* and *relevance*, as developed by psychologists, have been adopted by the Church in its approach to this sensitive area of psychological testing and screening.

Informed Consent

Psychologist Anne Anastasi has defined the three components of informed consent: the psychological test examinee should be informed of and knowledgeable about (1) the purpose of the testing, (2) the kind of data sought, and (3) the use that will be made of the results.[5] These criteria are particularly important when testing is provided for institutional purposes. John Ford even makes them mandatory for the validity of the tests administered: "Unless they [the examinees] have adequate, concrete knowledge of the uses to which the testing, evaluation and treatment are to be put, they do not give a valid consent to the proceedings."[6]

Obviously, the candidates cannot know the specific way in which the tests will yield certain results or the results could be jeopardized. But the candidate should have a "general but concrete appreciation of the kinds of material which these tests and interviews elicit and the kinds of reports which psychologists and psychiatrists make."[7] And, in addition to informing the individual as to the ethical standards of confidentiality that are imposed by the test giver's own professional societies, it would also be worthwhile for the client to know that the records of professionals can be subpoenaed in civil courts (although law and practice vary from state to state) and must be released under pain of contempt charges.[8]

Relevance

The principle of relevance is the practicable effort to ascertain the validity of tests or other psychological procedures for the particular diagnostic purposes for which they are being utilized. The information which the examined person is asked to reveal must be relevant to whatever has been stated as the purpose of the examination.

When a psychological evaluation is required by a religious community or a diocesan seminary for a potential candidate, can fulfillment of this requirement be used as carte blanche permission to investigate all areas of psychological functioning? W. C. Bier suggests that boundaries should be set before a psychologist begins an examination and that the clinician should resist "probing any more deeply into the personality of the subject than is really necessary to achieve the purpose of testing."[9] Any incursions that psychological inventories must make into the inner psyche should be made with reserve and restraint. Consequently, people whose professions place them in the position of having access to confidential information assume a serious obligation to obtain prior information about the nature and limits of confidentiality in those institutions (e.g., religious houses of formation, seminaries) that wish to employ their services.

There is an obvious "balance of rights" that needs to be identified in the questions of privacy and confidentiality. The religious community or diocese can best achieve this balance by preparing a sound policy on personnel records that incorporates principles of confidentiality for any psychological testing, including information about where the results of the tests are kept, who may have access to them, and for what period of time the tests will be kept. Just as important, religious communities, dioceses, and seminaries should be forthright in informing individuals of his or her rights in regards to confidentiality. As E. Rinere explains, justice would seem to indicate that a reasonable effort must be made by the institution:

> Certainly the primary responsibility for knowing one's rights lies with the individual, but justice dictates that an institute or other ecclesiastical body provide information if necessary. Unless a given individual is aware of these points on the right to privacy/confidentiality, he or she may be unjustly deprived of the right or may presume protection from it when no protection is actually available.[10]

Any medical records that might also be required pose additional concerns for the right of confidentiality. There are obvious ethical expectations placed upon physicians by their own profession to guard the privacy of their patients: "In general despite differences from state to state, federal laws protect the confidentiality of medical records, and information may not be disclosed without the patient's consent documented in writing by a special authorization form signed by the patient or the patient's legal representative."[11] Consent and confidentiality in regard to medical records become particularly important in such areas as substance-abuse treatment and HIV testing, which are subject to very stringent regulations on confidentiality. Rinere has summarized the dilemma over rights that emerges when such sensitive testing is required by an institute:

> If HIV or AIDS testing is a mandatory part of an admissions process, the candidate willingly agrees to the testing to achieve the desired goal; but the candidate should know beforehand how his or her right to privacy will be respected once the results are obtained. The candidate should clearly understand the role of these test results in the overall admission process.[12]

The individual who seeks to enter a seminary or religious community does not abandon his or her basic rights as now guaranteed by the Church in canon 220. "The individual willingly accepts the limitations associated with the canonical right for the sake of the common good, but hopefully not without complete initial understanding of what the right entails."[13]

Church Personnel Files and Confidentiality

Once a person becomes a member of a religious community or is accepted for ordination by the bishop of a diocese, a paper trail begins that will follow the individual for the rest of his or her time in that vocation. Commonly referred to as a "personnel file," this dossier may contain at any given time, as mentioned earlier, a plethora of information, including letters of complaints, commendations, and psychological and medical reports. No clear regulation about access to these records exists in the code of canon law except canon 220's general caution in regard to the rights to privacy and a good name.

The parameters for safeguarding privacy must therefore be left to particular law, that is, the law of the religious community or the diocese. Since the files of both religious and clerics may contain sensitive information, it is not unreasonable for a member of a religious community or a diocese to expect those who maintain his or her personnel file to have clear policies about who may have access and how long certain records are kept. Such protocols should also indicate the procedure for the individual's admittance to his or her own file, and what, if any, restrictions are placed upon such entry. "Superiors [of religious communities as well as diocesan bishops] under the banner of reverence for the individual and care for the common good, create, maintain and administer these [personnel] files in a spirit of discretion, justice and charity."[14]

Many diocesan bishops now request that religious superiors provide statements attesting to the presence or absence of any misconduct or improprieties in the records of members of religious institutes who wish to undertake ministry in the bishops' dioceses. In November 1993, the National Conference of Catholic Bishops approved a document called "Proposed Guidelines on the Assessment of Clergy and Religious for Assignment." The guidelines are recommended for use by religious superiors and bishops when a member of a religious community wishes to work in a particular diocese. The guidelines propose that the sending religious congregation review the work record of the candidate for ministry and provide relevant, prudent, and confidential exchange concerning the member's previous ministerial assignments. Information is also requested as to any seriously improper behavior, such as untreated substance abuse, violation of celibacy, sexual impropriety, physical abuse, or financial impropriety. In attempting to respond to such requests, it is important that religious congregations review their policies concerning the maintenance of personnel records and related issues of confidentiality.

A delicate balance must be scrupulously observed by all parties to the exchange: preserving the rights of the common good, namely, that the community be assigned worthy ministers who will never harm them; and preserving the rights of the individual to privacy and a good reputation. At times, there will be circumstances where the right of the individual to a good name must give way to the rights of the common good: "The injunction of the law is that no one *unlawfully* harm the good name of another. Thus there are circumstances in which the truth must be told and a good name lawfully harmed, so to speak."[15] But both sets of rights must be carefully monitored in each situation which involves potential ministerial opportunity. Granted, no canonical rights are absolute, in all circumstances, in every situation. Individual rights are always balanced with the rights of others and with the rights of the common good— "the sum of those conditions of social life which allow social groups and their individual members relatively thorough and ready access to their own fulfillment" (*Gaudium et Spes,* 26).

Bishops and superiors of religious communities are therefore called to a great sensitivity in the area of confidentiality. The bishop's or superior's careful sensitivity to the rights mentioned in canon 220 of the 1983 code that promote respect for privacy and the right to a good reputation will benefit the wider community and the individual priest or religious. But, in addition, the knowledge that one's psychic privacy and pertinent records will be respectfully treated can also serve to encourage an individual cleric or religious to seek professional assistance if it is ever desired or needed.

CHAPTER FIVE

The Annulment Process as a Ministry of Healing

IN THE LAST FEW YEARS, MANY PASTORAL MINISTERS HAVE explored new ways in which they may extend the Church's ministry of healing to Catholics who have experienced the tragedy of divorce. Pope John Paul II, in his "Apostolic Exhortation on the Family" reminded pastoral ministers of their serious responsibility to include within the faith community those who have suffered the tragedy of a failed marriage: "I earnestly call upon pastors and the whole community of the faithful to help the divorced and with solicitous care to make sure that they do not consider themselves as separated from the Church, for as baptized persons they can and indeed must share in her life."[1]

The Church proclaims through its magisterium the sacredness and sacramentality of the marriage bond in which Christian spouses mirror and give witness to Christ's union with his people. It has, at the same time, taken cognizance of the pain and anguish of the many who have not, for one reason or another, been able to live this teaching in its fullness.

The annulment process provided by the Church can be understood only within the broader context of the Church's marriage law.[2] This, in turn, requires an understanding of the Church's sacraments as encounters between the Lord and the believers within the community. Church law attempts to ensure the integrity of those encounters. For example, the sacrament of marriage is a unique interpersonal relationship between consenting parties who, in the presence of Christ, grant and accept certain mutual rights and responsibilities. Marriage law attempts to safeguard the integrity of this relationship, not only for the benefit of the parties themselves but for the benefit of the Christian community and the larger society as well.[3] This area of law includes establishing norms for marriage preparation, determining certain impediments, specifying the manner of consent and—if necessary, and sadly—adjudicating cases of marriage invalidity. As an instrument for discernment in this regard, the Church has for centuries utilized, with some modifications and developments, a legal institute known as the tribunal, or Church court.

A presumption of canon law is that all marriages brought to the tribunal for adjudication concerning possible invalidity are to be regarded as valid unless and until the contrary is proven.[4] An *annulment* is the declaration by the ecclesiastical tribunal that, contrary to what appears to be a valid marriage, a certain relationship does not fulfill the full legal requisites to be recognized as such by the ecclesial community.

A basic frame of reference for ecclesiastical courts is the Church's teaching on the indissolubility of marriage, which is understood to mean that a marriage once truly constituted may not be dissolved by any human authority. Of primary importance in assessing the validity of a particular marriage is the "consent" that was presumed to have been given by both parties. The Church securely identifies marriage with this mutual consent and declares that "no human power can replace this consent."[5] This teaching has been a traditional and basic tenet of Catholic theology and law. Over the centuries, the jurisprudence of Church courts has insisted that at least a minimal knowledge of what constitutes marriage must be present in both parties. There must be, in addition, a complete freedom from any pressures. These can be either external, as when a mother or father would adamantly insist that a son or daughter enter marriage because of an unplanned pregnancy, even when there is absolutely no desire or willingness on the part of the individual to give consent; or internal, such as grave fear. Moreover, before entering into marriage, a person must be capable of exercising normal human deliberation about the duties that he or she is called to undertake. In addition, the tribunal will examine the case to determine whether the teaching of Vatican II concerning the matrimonial covenant by which a man and woman establish between themselves a partnership for the whole of life has been operative in this particular union.

The process is a juridical one in which precise norms and procedures are followed to assist the court to determine the status of a particular marriage. Many personnel working in the typical tribunal also see their work as participation in a healing ministry, since the staff comes in direct contact with individuals whose lives have often been deeply scarred by their marriage experiences. As one such official has explained: "Tribunal personnel need to be aware of the fact that they are often dealing with people who are still hurting deeply, people who at times feel very alienated from the Church, people who are laden with a great deal of guilt."[6] Pastoral ministers who must deal with a wide spectrum of suffering people in this same context—many times assisting in the preparation of tribunal papers—need also to identify their assistance in terms of Jesus' healing ministry.

Other helping professions have much to offer the Church, especially in identifying some of the dynamics at work in the divorced or divorcing person who comes forward to seek an ecclesiastical annulment. Familiarity with such insights may be useful in helping the minister to deal in a constructive way with the pain experienced by the petitioner. The famed Dr. Elizabeth Kübler-Ross, for instance, broke new ground a number of years ago in identifying the various stages an individual passes through when facing a terminal illness.[7] Her analysis can provide a helpful paradigm for the person who is undergoing the breakdown of a marriage: shock, denial, anger, bargaining, depression, acceptance can all be stages of a person's journey out of a broken marriage.[8]

We have no way of knowing ahead of time at what stage of grief an inquiring party in an annulment procedure may be when he or she approaches the pastoral minister. As Power explains, these people come with a variety of pastoral circumstances and problems which may need to be addressed:

Very often people who approach the Tribunal [as well as the parish minister] are more than one-time losers. Not only have they had dreams shattered by a broken marriage, but often as they reveal their life-history, they speak of their parents' unhappy and possibly violent marriage, of childhood trauma, sexual abuse, of earlier broken romances, of exploitation. The story of the relationship and marriage in question can be filled with every kind of human suffering.[9]

For the Catholic petitioner this pain is frequently magnified: there is often the recognition of personal failure in not having lived up to the perceived expectations of the Church in regards to the sanctity and permanence of marriage.

Some tribunals utilize an extensive questionnaire to assist the petitioner in preparing the formal petition for the annulment. The parish minister can be extremely helpful in reviewing with the petitioner this documentation which can at first appear unduly cumbersome, even intimidating. Perhaps most disconcerting for the potential applicant for annulment is the requirement that one review in depth many aspects of one's life and family background, recounting in detail one's upbringing, one's relationship to parents and siblings, the extensive history of the dating, courtship and marriage, and the actual breakdown of the marital relationship. Naturally, there is an apprehension about sharing such a personal journey and the painful memories that may be dredged up. But, as many who have begun and successfully completed this process have found, there can be a sense of wholeness and redemption, as they put loose ends together and place anger into perspective. As they write their marriage history, many begin to see, for the first time, some connections and patterns between the features of their early years and the problems that later emerged and perhaps affected the formative years of their marriage. The questionnaire facilitates this awareness by presenting a chronological ordering which invites the individual to see his or her life experiences worked out over a number of years, and to see that the failure of the marriage is most likely not due to one particular event or circumstance.

One petitioner applying for an annulment commented on the impact that filling out the questionnaire had on his spiritual life: "Yes, the process is very personal and as such is very painful. But for the emotionally and spiritually wounded Catholic trying to find meaning in the pain of divorce, the annulment process offers a special form of relief."[10] He goes on to share his appreciation for the many ways in which he was affected: "First, the process is an instrument of forgiveness and reconciliation. Second, it is excellent preparation for a second marriage. And third, it promotes a new understanding of the role grace plays in a sacramental marriage."[11] For many like this applicant, the procedure puts the past into a new and growth-filled perspective:

> By seeing a marriage as seriously flawed from the beginning (the church's definition of an invalid marriage), the ex-partners can put their tremendous emotional pain into perspective. The cruelty that seems absurd becomes much more understandable. The particular behavior of the former spouse that triggered so much anger and anguish becomes less important. The simple statement that comes at the end of the annulment process says it all: there were conditions that prevented the spouses from making a binding commitment.[12]

The procedure can thus facilitate a peaceful parting. "By the end of the annulment process, the ex-partners should be in a much better position to recognize that their prime failing was a lack of commitment. They should find it easier to forgive each other for the hurtful behavior that results automatically when two people attempt to build an intimate relationship on a flawed foundation."[13]

The importance of the Church to the divorced person at this time in his/her life cannot be overstated. The message of God's faithful love which is present throughout one's life needs to be especially articulated to include the feelings of powerlessness which the experience of divorce can engender. Many will be undergoing a "grieving" of the loss of a relationship that has had great significance for them, even if it has also been the source of great pain. "Few realize that they are grieving the loss not of one relationship, but many. Lack of understanding of grief causes many to say: 'Not only have I lost my marriage but now I'm losing my mind'. They need to be reassured that what they are experiencing is 'normal.'"[14]

Two qualities are necessary for the grieving person: gentleness and patience with oneself. "These virtues, together with an understanding that the grieving ranges in time from two to five years, are important in healing the unrealistic expectations that plague a person who says: 'Why am I still crying? I ought to be over this by now.'"[15]

Research done a few years ago in Rochester, New York, tested the belief that in the person undergoing a divorce some universal personal fears can be identified which characterize the traumatic effect. One survey question completed by divorced Catholics related to the participants' perception of "their most pressing problems at present":[16]

Problems	Response
Loneliness	53%
Dating and Intimate Relationships	48%
Financial Difficulties	38%
Fears of the Future	36%
Fears of Remarriage	33%
Parenting Problems	30%
Relations with Former Spouse	23%

The pervasive presence of so many sources of anxiety during the divorce experience indicates that an individual may not be ready psychologically to begin the annulment process. J. Frederico sees many changes in thought patterns within the divorcing and divorced person, including what he terms a "period of transition" in which the person asks the question: "I am about to be divorced—what do I do now?"[17] This period is an acute phase of coping wherein the individual must face such fears as change in income, a possible change in living arrangements, and altered relationships with children and in-laws, as well as such uncertain factors as the children's adjustment to this situation, single dating, the long-term mental consequences, etc. During this stage persons continually mull over their fears and their new situations. "It is as if there is an unceasing mental review of the divorcing person's present situation plus all its implications."[18] It is often observed that people experiencing this transition period express the feeling that they are in "a tunnel with no light at the end, but that the tunnel may be a long one."[19]

Although the question of an annulment may be raised during this period, it is important to see "where the person is at" as he or she contemplates the decision whether or not to apply. The person may be at a "blaming stage," and his or her account of the causes of the divorce may tend to lay major responsibility on the other spouse. Frederico would call this the "first degree" account, that stage in which there has been no time or opportunity to put the events leading to divorce into any perspective and thus the account is simplistic. In what he describes as a "second degree" account the person develops an awareness of the shared responsibility or features of both partners that may have led to the divorce. "This kind of an account tends to emerge farther along the adjustment process—after the initial wave of hurt has subsided, and after the person has had time to reflect on his or her own behavior."[20] The "third degree" account emerges after the period of transition, at the point when the person no longer feels bonded to the past but looks to the future and new relationships and is interested in seeing the marriage for what it can teach.

It may be possible in listening to the accounts given by the individual to assess his or her readiness to begin the annulment procedure. It seems reasonable, in the absence of indications to the contrary, to infer that the person who displays a rather clear-cut first-degree account is probably not ready to begin the process. Since the second-degree account indicates an appreciation of interdependent influences on the divorce, it may indicate a better possibility of follow through on the part of the potential applicant. Obviously, those who reveal a third-degree account probably have the greatest level of emotional readiness for entering and successfully completing the annulment process.

Helpful Hints

Pastoral ministers who have patience and due respect for the privacy of each individual who comes forward wishing to begin the annulment process will more easily bring about healing and reconciliation. There are several steps the parish minister can take to help facilitate the process:

1. Know, at least in a general way, the ecclesiastical procedures that are used in the annulment process, since the individual approaching will have several questions about the procedure—how

long it will take, what the person will need to submit, who will have to participate, and so on. Tribunal staff are usually more than willing to meet with parish staff members to review and explain tribunal procedures and answer questions. In addition, many tribunals provide helpful written materials that summarize many pertinent details about the procedure. Mention could also be made that the annulment process is not related formally to the civil divorce procedures (questions concerning legitimacy, child support, custody, change of surname for the ex-wife and possibly children, etc.), nor does it deal with apportioning responsibility—legal, canonical, or moral. It is not a fault-finding process and does not declare anyone "guilty."

Strictly speaking, the annulment process is first and foremost a church *legal* process that resolves a canonical question regarding the possible invalidity of a given marriage. There is never an implicit guarantee beforehand that an affirmative decision will be given regarding possible invalidity. In fact, as we have seen, the presumption of the law is that the marriage is valid. The petitioner should know that the former spouse must, by law, be contacted, although annulments can proceed in some circumstances without the participation of the respondent, and that several witnesses will be needed. The case may take several months or more, and the petitioner should expect to pay the tribunal for the court costs that will be needed to process the case.

2. Listen for opportunities to begin a healing process. Many come to the Church after divorce seeing the annulment process as a negative experience that will have no personal value beyond the legal purposes for which it was created. But over the years many in tribunal work have seen new dimensions of healing that can be initiated by the legal process and can flow along with it. Moreover, people come forward to begin this process with different emotional levels and significantly different experiences of divorce. A listening, nonjudgmental posture which allows the petitioner the opportunity to discuss some of the attendant strains and doubts of his or her experience can help make the interview a compassionate channel of healing and growth.

3. Gently invite the person to accountability. Once the petitioner is aware of the process for annulment and the personal history that will be required, a great potential for avoidance and procrastina-

tion exists. Many pastoral ministers, after reviewing with the applicant the procedures and questionnaire, suggest a follow-up meeting where the completed questionnaire can be returned with the pertinent documentation such as baptismal certificate(s), divorce papers, etc. This second meeting can also allow for an extended discussion about some of the areas of personal adjustment to divorce which may have previously surfaced. "Filing a successful annulment petition requires reflection, communication and organization. In other words, the individual must accept responsibility for managing the process."[21]

A trained family therapist with a background in canon law has commented on the potential of the annulment procedure for positive growth: "I see the Church as a mediator of relational care. In helping people look fairly at their own relationships, vertical and horizontal, the Church assures itself of having a healthy, thriving relationship with the individual."[22] Andrew McDonald, bishop of Little Rock, Arkansas, in a homily addressed to tribunal officials (and in a way, to all who work with the divorced), assigned them a wonderful mission and vision of ministry:

> Eagerly share information, keep people up-to-date, give them hope, let your tribunals be an instrument of peace and reconciliation in the lives of the wounded so that 'the last shall be first and the first last'.[23]

Pastoral ministers who work with the divorced and have a basic knowledge of tribunal procedures and canon law can be a channel of grace and healing for many who come forward wounded and in need of knowing God's mercy and peace.

CHAPTER SIX

Walking Together:
The Diocesan Synod

THE DIOCESE OF ROCHESTER IS A MEDIUM-SIZED DIOCESE with approximately 350,000 Roman Catholics and covers twelve counties and 7,107 square miles in upstate New York. Bernard J. McQuaid, a driving conservative force in the ecclesiastical battles that raged in the Church in America in the nineteenth and early twentieth centuries, was the first bishop and began his episcopal ministry in 1868 when the diocese was founded.

On May 2, 1979, Matthew H. Clark, a native of the Diocese of Albany, New York, was named Rochester's eighth bishop. Like many dioceses in the United States since the Second Vatican Council, Rochester has struggled with many controversial issues, including the clergy shortage and the role of women in the Church. In 1991, after consultation with the presbyteral council (or priest's senate) as required by law, Clark issued a summons to the local church to embark on a diocesan synod to be held in two years and in conjunction with the 125th anniversary of the founding of the diocese.

In convoking the synod (*syn* + *hodos*, "with" and "road," to "journey with") Clark was utilizing an ancient canonical institute that has been a part of the Church from earliest times and has been adapted for use in a variety of forms for several centuries. Since promulgation of the 1983 code there has been a renewed interest in diocesan synods as a way to facilitate broad-based planning and to develop legislation in the local church.

The history of the diocesan synod is very much linked with the history of regional (or provincial) synods. When Roman persecution of the Church came to an end in the fourth century, bishops began to assemble, often accompanied by some of their clergy, to discuss common concerns and strategies. By the end of the fourth century, the custom of conducting provincial synods became fairly well established in the Eastern Church, especially as a means of sharing counsel from the mother church to the newer churches being formed.[1]

A slightly different set of circumstances in the West led to the development of diocesan synods. In the early centuries it was common for the clergy of an area to live in close proximity to the bishop; such proximity was conducive to their gathering to discuss matters of concern and to the formulation of common pastoral practice. As the Church grew and pastoral service to the more rural areas was needed, it became increasingly more common for presbyters to be located in rural districts, separated from the cathedral and the bishop. But to ensure that all the priests of a region would know of recent legislation and would be prepared to battle against unorthodox practices or schisms, bishops began assembling priests periodically for formal meetings at the cathedral which ultimately became identified as diocesan synods.

By the seventh century the practice of convoking synods had multiplied throughout the Western Church and provincial councils were issuing legislation requiring the convening of diocesan synods in their regions. These synods followed provincial synods and provided the opportunity to discuss new ecclesiastical regulations.[2] By the eleventh century, synods had become so common that ceremonial norms were developed with liturgical formularies that specified "three or four days of meetings with set scripture readings, defined prayers, and sermons at appropriate times."[3]

Although diocesan synods were held frequently during the Middle Ages, their frequent usage had an unfortunate and negative side effect: they became routine, with passive participation on the part of the attending clergy. With the Reformation and external and internal demands for reform of the Church, the Council of Trent reasserted the importance of synods and ordered their annual celebration in each diocese. Subsequently, until the seventeenth century, synods were again routinely conducted as a means of applying the teachings and canons of the Council of Trent.

After a period of some decline, the nineteenth century saw an increased awareness of the benefits of the diocesan synod. Pope Pius IX reminded bishops of their canonical obligation to conduct synods and of the reinvigorating possibilities of such assemblies in the diocesan church. Regulations about synods were also slated to be discussed at the First Vatican Council (1869), but the draft proposed was never considered. The 1917 code legislated that diocesan synods be held in every diocese every ten years, but few dioceses observed this requirement.

The 1983 code has reemphasized the importance of the diocesan synod, and here the concept has been revamped as a result of the added theological underpinnings of the new ecclesiology of the Second Vatican Council. The orientation of the council towards understanding the Church as the "People of God," with all members sharing in the responsibility to evangelize, gives a new dimension to the gathering of the Church in a synod. *Lumen Gentium* insists that all in the Church form a "messianic people" and have a unique contribution to make to the life of the Church.[4] Thus canon 460 speaks of the diocesan synod as a "group of selected priests and other Christian faithful of a particular Church which offers assistance to the diocesan bishop for the good of the entire diocesan community." The format for such assistance can vary. But it is clear that many bishops are using the synod for more than a purely legislative forum, for example, for diocesan planning efforts, or to address any needs pertaining to the diocesan church that could be facilitated by widespread consultation. *The Directory on the Pastoral Ministry of Bishops* (1973), which preceded the code, gave some practical recommendations for synodal activity and described the synod as an event of "extraordinary importance" wherein the bishop might adapt the laws and norms of the universal church to local conditions, clarify the policies and programs of apostolic work in the diocese, as well as correct errors in doctrine and morals if needed.[5]

One of the major advances of the new legislation, reflecting the increased participation of all the faithful in the life of the local church, is the expansion of the membership of the diocesan synod beyond the clergy. Canon 463 §2 legislates the active participation at the synod of lay members of the Christian faithful. This inclusion is a natural recognition of the rightful participation of the lay Christian faithful in the affairs of the Church and of the importance of including their gifts and experience in the synodal deliberations. Moreover, the code provides the opportunity to invite members of other ecclesial communities to attend as observers, a reminder of a similar type of participation by such representatives at Vatican II.

The canons of the code do not specifically address the manner of celebrating the synod. This is left to the discretion of the diocesan bishop, presumably in collaboration with the synod members and with local diocesan liturgical personnel.

The *Directory on the Pastoral Ministry of Bishops* also recommended that a preparatory commission be established prior to an actual synod.[6] This hearkens back to the work of similar commissions that prepared materials for the bishops who gathered for the Second Vatican Council. Such preliminary work is vital, if a synod is to be a productive exchange, since concrete proposals based on wide consultation should be drawn up to provide focus and significant material for synod discussions.

It is clear from canon 466 that at a diocesan synod the bishop acts as the sole legislator, i.e., he ultimately determines which if any of the deliberations or recommendations that flow from the synodal gathering will be considered as "law" for the diocese.[7] Although it is clear that he cannot delegate this important responsibility (legislating), it is also clear that the very nature of a synod—a "walking together" of the local church—presumes wide consultation and the bishop's careful listening to whatever action steps might be proposed. In fact, the synod members enjoy a "consultative vote" involving a juridic collaboration and more than just the giving of "advice." It will, in fact, be extremely difficult to engage people in future collaborative efforts in a diocese if it does not appear that the insights and recommendations that were gathered in the course of a synod experience have been fairly and thoroughly considered. While the right of the Church to ensure good order is protected by stipulating that the bishop is the only legislator, another traditional canonical principle states that those who are affected by the law should participate in its formulation.[8] Thus sensitivity on the part of the bishop helps to insure that the legislation and programs that emerge as a result of the synod deliberations are practically and correctly addressing the true pastoral needs of the diocese, not imagined or illusionary ones.

A Practical Experience: A Synod in Rochester

In June 1991, Bishop Matthew Clark announced, after consultation with the presbyteral council, that he wished to convoke a synod for the Diocese of Rochester, to take place in October of 1993. This gathering of delegates of the local church would also be the occasion for the celebration of the 125th anniversary of the founding of the diocese.

The last synod in Rochester had been held in 1954. It was celebrated in the cathedral and, typical of the mores of the Church at that time, only the bishop and the priests of the diocese were in attendance. Also indicative of a former ecclesiology, there had been no prior consultation as to the content of the synodal legislation. A book of new rules for the diocese (primarily directed toward diocesan clergy) had been prepared by the chancery staff and was distributed at the synodal gathering.[9] The priests received the legislation at the synod and were then promptly (yet ceremoniously!) asked to vote for its promulgation; the motion passed, as expected, unanimously.

But by 1990, an entirely new approach to synods had emerged, as previously discussed, in the post–Vatican II Church and as now legislated in the 1983 code. Underscoring the need for broad-based consultation in preparation for a synod, Bishop Clark in the spring of 1990 sent a survey instrument (see appendix) to all registered Catholics in the twelve-county diocese. The responses, as Clark explained in a cover letter, would help form the agenda for the actual synod deliberations, which would, in turn, help to guide the diocese into the new millennium.

In addition, he appointed Father Joseph Hart, a theology professor at St. Bernard's Institute in Rochester, as director of the synod, and Marcy Holtz, a religious education administrator in the diocese, as associate director. He then appointed twenty-four members of the diocese—clergy, religious, and laity—to a synod commission which would advise and assist Father Hart in developing the operational details of the synodal "process."

With the support and encouragement of Clark, the commission planned a highly consultative synod procedure. In the fall of 1992 and the spring of 1993, each local faith community would hold its own "synod." The results of all of the parish synods were collected, summarized, and discussed regionally, by delegates to the general synod from each of the parishes of the region (or pastoral zone). Finally, the recommendations from all eleven regions of the diocese were prioritized and then discussed at the general synod with delegates from throughout the diocese, gathered at a convention center in downtown Rochester.

At the conclusion of the general synod, the recommendations were presented to Bishop Clark for approval and promulgation. A synod implementation commission was then formed to shepherd the recommendations into reality.

Almost 20,000 Catholics in the diocese responded to the initial survey. On the basis of the information gathered, Bishop Clark chose six themes later developed into position papers that served as the resources for the synod discussions. The questions addressed in the papers were as follows:

- How can we as a Church help strengthen Christian marriage and family life in all its forms?
- How can we support our parishes in being faith-filled, celebrating communities?
- How can we help those facing unwanted pregnancy or terminal illness?
- How can we meet the special needs of youth and young adults, as well as the elderly and those who care for them?
- How can we improve our efforts in faith development and in inviting others to share the Gospel of Jesus Christ?
- How can we do the work of justice, combating racism, sexism, poverty, unemployment, and the lack of affordable housing and health care?

It was the hope of Bishop Clark that, through the synod, the parishes and communities would, in a concrete way, experience their coresponsibility for the Church of Rochester and its mission, and help to prioritize needs while planning for the future.

After the six themes had been discerned, writing committees were assembled consisting of nine to eleven members, each committee including a local theologian, a specialist with expertise related to the theme, and a writer who was responsible for preparing the document that would serve as the basis for discussion by the parish synods. These six documents synthesized pertinent scriptural and church teachings and other materials related to the theme into practicable discussion tools. The papers also included recommendations about how the Church of Rochester could begin to meet those needs.

In preparation for the parish and regional synod meetings, teams of five parishioners from each of the parishes of the diocese attended training sessions so they would be able to facilitate the parish synods in their own faith communities. Included in their job description were handling publicity, distributing synod material, helping to select delegates to the regional and general synods from the parish, and making the necessary physical arrangements in their respective parishes.

In the fall of 1992, each parish gathered its members, in as many sessions as could be arranged to accommodate the various schedules of parishioners, to discuss the synod materials. The papers distributed to all parishioners before the meetings presented such topics as marriage and family life, the parish community, violence, addiction, unwanted pregnancy, and terminal illness. Each parish then made some concrete recommendations about how the diocese could improve its ministry in these areas. These recommendations were forwarded to the regional meetings after they had been collated and listed according to rankings generated in the parishes.

In the fall of 1992 and again in the spring of 1993, synod delegates gathered at the regional level to discuss and rank the results of the parish synods. At each of the regional meetings, the delegates worked in small discussion groups and were asked to reflect on the forty-five recommendations that had surfaced from the parish sessions throughout the diocese. In the fall, by weighted voting, the regional delegates chose the five most important recommendations in each of three theme categories: "marriage and family life," "faith-filled, celebrating communities," and "violence, addiction, burdensome pregnancy, and terminal illness." In the spring, regional gatherings reconvened to discuss and rank recommendations in the final three categories: "youth, young adults, the elderly and those who care for them," "problems in faith development and evangelization," and "challenges of justice: racism, sexism, poverty, unemployment, homelessness and health care."

What then emerged were thirty recommendations (fifteen from fall and fifteen from spring) which formed the agenda for the seventh general synod held on October 1–3, 1993 at the Rochester Riverside Convention Center. Over 1,500 delegates from all over the diocese gathered to reflect on practical and concrete proposals for the life of the Church of Rochester. These proposals had their roots in the 1990 survey of 129,000 Catholic households. From these roots the parish and regional synod discussions had produced recommendations in each theme category which were given a final priority by the general synod. This assembly would choose the top three recommendations from each of the theme categories and then select five which would form the backbone of a pastoral plan, to guide the Church of Rochester into the twenty-first century.

In December 1993, Bishop Clark issued a pastoral plan for the diocese containing five goals based on the recommendations of the general synod:

1. Form Catholics in beliefs, traditions, and values throughout life;
2. Advocate for a consistent life ethic;
3. Teach the Catholic moral tradition;
4. Recognize and value the dignity of women in Church and society;
5. Promote the growth of small Christian communities.

The second leading vote-getter at the general synod—promoting a consistent life ethic—was not on the original list of recommendations that had surfaced during the deliberations of the parish and the regional synods. However, through the grace and power of the Spirit present at the general synod, an opportunity was provided for delegates to recommend priorities that might have somehow been overlooked or inadvertently muted.

Each of the five summary goals announced by the bishop was accompanied by specific action steps to implement the goal. But rather than delegate the specific activity that each parish would undertake, the diocesan administrative offices would assist in whatever way they could, providing services that would help implement the various programs chosen by the parishes. To help facilitate this follow-up, Bishop Clark named a full-time staff person to help oversee the implementation. In addition, nearly fifty people were invited to participate in interdisciplinary teams charged with developing annual work plans that would support implementation of the pastoral plan.

Throughout the diocese the response to the synod experience was overwhelmingly positive. As Bishop Clark noted in issuing the resulting pastoral plan: "Throughout this journey we have benefited from the rich streams of faith, diversity, imagination, and talent with which our gracious God has endowed us. The hallmark of our Synod process has been open, honest dialogue guided by the Holy Spirit."[10]

While the notion of a diocesan synod has remained stable, the means for carrying it out have varied from age to age. Diocesan synods truly reflect the ecclesiologies of the Church operative at particular times in its history. Synods today can involve, at various stages, the participation of the entire local church. As promoted by the 1983 *Code of Canon Law,* the diocesan synod is no longer restricted to presbyteral gatherings with the bishop where "pro-forma" affirmation is given to local legislation which has never been seen by the participants before the synodal gathering. The diocesan synod has thus become a special grace for the whole local church.

CHAPTER SEVEN

A Reconciling Church:
Alternative Dispute Resolution

CONFLICT IS ALMOST INEVITABLE WITHIN A SOCIETY ENGAGED in communication and interaction. The cultural conditioning in Western society tends to negate the value of conflict and suppresses feelings associated with conflict. Although conflict may be negative (when, for example, it results from a hostile desire to destroy) it can also be positive—when it results from a desire or will to heal, or to unite, or to improve. Alternative dispute resolution methods have evolved as an effort to transform conflict through a process of self-awareness that opens the possibility of personal growth and healing within the individual and healing ultimately within the larger community.

One possible area for conflict that has emerged over the recent centuries is the question of rights. As we have seen, one of the new developments in the revised code of canon law is the specification of rights and obligations for all the Christian faithful. But the mere acknowledgment of rights will have little value if there is no clear way in which these rights can be vindicated and sustained. How do we hold each other and the institutional Church accountable for the safeguarding of rights? If we do not have effective and credible procedures for the protection of rights, the worry of the American statesman Alexander Hamilton will seem applicable: "All the reservation of particular rights or privileges would amount to nothing."[1]

The right of the members of the Church to seek redress of grievances can be traced to Jesus himself, who said that when conflicts arise between his followers and cannot be resolved by them, they should be referred to witnesses or to the community for resolution (Matt. 18: 15–18). St. Paul admonished the early Christians to resolve their differences but to do so within the Church community and not to utilize civil court proceedings. Hence, by the second century the Church had developed a judicial system for dispute resolution. The *Didiscalia Apostolorum* (third century), with its precise regulations detailing court procedures, gives some indication of the need experienced early in the Church to develop some measures for the protection of rights. Emperor Constantine granted to bishops civil powers to judge cases. This occasioned the utilization of Roman civil law in ecclesiastical courts, which, in turn, profoundly influenced ecclesiastical jurisprudence for centuries.

From the Middle Ages until the early twentieth century, aggrieved parties could appeal administrative acts and juridical decisions to their metropolitan tribunal[2] or to the Roman Rota, but in 1908 Pope Pius X limited administrative recourse against decisions of a bishop to the congregations of the Roman curia.[3] By the time of the 1917 code, judicial procedures included provisions for an independent judiciary, the right of the individual to be represented by an advocate, the right to a speedy trial, and other protections.

Rather than utilize trial procedures, civil law as well as recent canon law has looked to "due process" as a way of resolving conflicts. The search for new ways to deal with conflict resolution within the civil sphere has been propelled for the most part by ever-escalating court costs. Some would even blame these prohibitive costs on the inherent weaknesses of the modern trial for such a problem: "The elaborate procedures of the adversary system are precisely the reason that legal services are so expensive and beyond the reach of most ordinary citizens."[4]

Correspondingly, there has been a movement in the Church towards conciliation procedures, but from a different motivation. Canon 221 §1 states that the Christian faithful enjoy the right to "legitimately vindicate and defend the rights which they enjoy before a competent ecclesiastical forum in accord with the norm of law." While the internal judicial procedures for remedies can sometimes be seen as cumbersome and time-consuming, canon law itself encourages parties to turn first to alternative forms of dispute settlement, when they are available to resolve differences, before considering more formal court procedures. The judge, according to canon 1446 §2, is "not to neglect to encourage the parties to collaborate in working out an equitable solution . . . perhaps even employing the services of reputable persons for mediation." According to canon 1446 §1, all the Christian faithful are to "avoid lawsuits . . . as much as possible and resolve them peacefully as soon as possible."

Conciliation and arbitration are two of the primary forms of alternative dispute resolution which are utilized by both civil law and church communities today. Conciliation can be understood as "an informal process in which a third party tries to bring the disagreeing parties to some agreement by lowering tensions, improving communication, interpreting issues, providing technical assistance, exploring potential solutions and bringing about a negotiated settlement, either informally or in a subsequent step, through formal mediation."[5] Arbitration is understood as the "submission of a dispute to a third party who renders a decision after hearing arguments and reviewing evidence."[6] Although the elements utilized in these processes are adapted from secular models, they should have distinct differences within the Church: "Conciliation, in the context of being an alternative dispute resolution in the church, essentially involves Christian notions of forgiveness, peace-making and fraternal charity."[7]

In the United States diocesan mediation boards have been available since the early 1970s, but for a variety of reasons they seem to have been generally ineffective; in some dioceses they have never even been utilized.[8] Many reasons are suggested for this phenomenon. Some claim that many people have been unaware of the existence of a conciliation process in the diocese. Still others note that many of the Christian faithful have been ignorant of their rights and therefore have not sought their vindication. It is also possible that those who exercise administrative authority have been less than enthusiastic about making such procedures available, perhaps knowing that they themselves might be summoned to a proceeding initiated by a party with a grievance. There is also the problem of sufficient personnel to provide these procedures, since the obvious resource for this work is the marriage tribunal in a diocese, whose staff is often, however, unavailable to take on such an assignment due to the burden of numerous marriage cases. Perhaps one of the greatest obstacles to the success of alternative methods of resolution has been the refusal of respondents who are cited to participate in a conciliation procedure. As R. Bass asks: "[S]ince conciliation and arbitration are both voluntary processes, what if the person who allegedly occasions the rights violation chooses not to participate? . . . What should be done?"[9] Unfortunately such questions have thus far been left largely unanswered.

For all these reasons, the growth of Church-sponsored conciliation procedures has been slow and uneven. But some hopeful developments are taking place. J. Coriden has presented some possibilities taken from secular models of Alternative Dispute Resolution (ADR) that can be adapted for use in the Church. One such possibility is the use of an "ombudsman," a third party who regularly receives and investigates complaints or grievances aimed at an institution by its constituents, clients, or employees. "The ombudsman may take actions such as bringing an apparent injustice to the attention of high level officials, advising a settlement of the dispute or proposing systematic changes in the institution."[10]

As Coriden has suggested, there are many advantages to utilizing alternate dispute resolution methods which can make them attractive to the Church:

1. There is personal involvement on the part of the individuals, and the conflict is not placed in the hands of lawyers.
2. The results of the process may be more appropriate to the specific situation that gave rise to the conflict than the results achieved in court might be.
3. Perhaps most desirable, the context for the process may be less adversarial than the court setting, which is designed for adversarial efforts to achieve resolution.
4. Christian values such as reconciliation can be the basis for both the process and the desired result.[11]

A broad range and large number of conflicts arise within the local church on a regular basis—disputes between pastors and parish councils, questions about the inadmission of persons to sacraments, issues between pastors and parish staffs—many of which could be resolved with the assistance of Alternative Dispute Resolution procedures. Dioceses should consider establishing offices that could offer such services and assist in such problematic situations. These alternative processes might even be established as mandatory, in the sense that "the parties would be estopped from access to the diocesan tribunal, hierarchic recourse[12] or other more formal due process or grievance procedures until this ADR process was attempted in good faith and found wanting."[13]

Success will be one of the best advertisements for promoting the use of ADR in a diocese. "If the process can earn a reputation for quick, fair and low-cost settlements . . . then people will use it willingly."[14]

A major educational effort should be undertaken so that everyone in the diocese is aware that such procedures are available, knows the benefit of such processes, and has access to the names and phone numbers of those who operate the process. It will also be helpful to distribute brochures and to conduct conferences and workshops on a fairly frequent basis, since people may need to be reminded of these avenues available for resolving Church conflicts. Priests especially must be educated to such procedures since they may occasionally be cited as participants by parishioners or staff members who feel themselves aggrieved. In some dioceses, human resource offices provide procedures and personnel for employee-related conflicts. But in some dioceses there is no clear-cut process for resolving such tensions, and, sadly, employees often leave service in the Church frustrated and bitter, or take their complaints to the secular courts for resolution.

The benefits of utilizing conciliation procedures are plentiful. For many people, the cost of obtaining justice through the civil court system is high. In most cases, mediation services are free or at least very reasonable. Often, disputes to be resolved in courts are backlogged for long periods. Mediation cases are usually heard shortly after the disputes arise. Perhaps most important, free from the usual rules of civil court procedures and processes, disputants in conciliation, with the assistance of trained mediators, can get to the root causes of a dispute. Once given the opportunity to state their own case fully, they are usually better able to hear the other party's point of view. Such an airing of grievances can positively mend relationships among families, friends, parishioners, pastoral staffs, and others who make up our Church communities.

As Coriden has realistically stated, "[A]DR is not a panacea. It will not eliminate sin or human cussedness. We must not expect too much from it. Some people don't want their disputes settled. Sometimes a good compromise leaves both parties unsatisfied. And sometimes the most that can be accomplished is a sense of having been heard, of having had one's day in court. That alone could make ADR worth a try."[15]

Epilogue

HOWARD HAS ARGUED THAT IN THE AMERICAN LEGAL SYSTEM overregulation directed toward making law "more scientific," thus creating uniformity and denying any need for human judgment, has failed. The efforts to remove all ambiguity from our lives have not resulted in the intended goal. Precise regulations imply a certain necessity that everything should look alike.[1] What results is an elaborate complex of regulations which allow for no variance or deviation, no role for human judgment, all of which is much to the disadvantage of the group or business that is being regulated. What seems to be missing from the equation is humanity: "[I]ncreasingly, law makes us feel like victims. We divert our energies into defensive measures designed solely to avoid tripping over rules that seem to exist only because someone put them there."[2] The result of all this can be a mindless preoccupation not with the values that triggered the legislation but with regulating itself. "Law itself, not the goals to be advanced by law, is now our focus. Indeed, the main lesson of law without judgment is that law's original goal is lost."[3]

Law has become enshrined in the social fabric of the United States as the great protector of all that we hold sacred in a democracy. Law is often rightly hailed as the instrument of freedom. Without law, there would be anarchy. However, too much law, we are learning, can have a negative effect.

So too within the Catholic legal tradition. It is easy to make the same criticisms. If Catholics believe that they are called to a conformity under laws that, in most instances, they have had little opportunity to affect or inform, the same criticisms will be made.

Any change in perspective about Church law will have to come first from those who administer the law in the Church: administrators, tribunal judges, canon lawyers. C. Mooney quotes Thomas Shaffer: "Lawyers do not, most of the time 'dispense' or 'administer' or serve justice. They serve people who know and who want to know how to live together."[4] While Shaffer is speaking of lawyers in general, his principle also applies to the legal procedures of the Church. Our own canonical system must be perceived as encapsulating the values of a community that wants to live together in union with Jesus Christ.

The code of canon law can help us to see ourselves as disciples of the Lord, belonging to a family and trying to do what Jesus did—to teach, to heal, to overcome evil.[5] "The awareness that all Christians are called to be disciples of Christ is, indeed, one of the signs of the times. However, Catholics have not been reminded enough of this basic call. . . . There are signs implicitly of this call to discipleship in the code and explicitly in the documents of the council."[6]

As a guide to pastoral ministry, Church law functions best when it helps to provide peace to the community so that the mission of discipleship among all the members can be facilitated. "Belonging to this pastoral ministry is the providing for the messianic peace which Christ came to give. There can be no peace without law. The absence of law, or the existence of antiquated or unjust laws is an invitation to chaos."[7] The goal of law in providing a service to the community is not the multiplication of regulations, precepts, and statutes. Rather it is to bring harmony and peace to the community so the Church's values can be maintained:

> The Scriptural word *shalom* sums up all the blessings of the messianic kingdom. Shalom is more than tranquillity of order, as Augustine describes peace. Rather, it is the order that comes from the inner ordering of persons to one another, through their relationship to God. It seems . . . that the beatitude "Blessed are the peacemakers," applies in a special way to those who devote themselves to canon law.[8]

Canon law assists the community when it can identify the various gifts that come from the Spirit and suggest how they can be utilized to build up the Church. "Canon law reminds us that there really is a variety of gifts with the same spirit, and that difference of gifts is not privilege but varying responsibilities to build up the Body of Christ."[9]

Synodal Survey,
Diocese of Rochester

SETTING THE SYNOD AGENDA

Please take a few minutes to fill out this survey to help us identify the themes and issues you feel should be taken up by the 1993 Synod of the Diocese of Rochester. The Synod, through a series of meetings, will help to set the direction for the future of the Church in this area so your contribution is very important.

PREPARANDO LOS TEMAS DEL SINODO

Por favor, llene esta encuesta para ayudarnos a identificar los temas y problemas que usted cree que se deben discutir en el Sínodo de la Dióesis de Rochester que se celebará en 1993. El Sínodo, por medio de una serie de reuniones, ayudará a determinar el rumbo que debe tomar la Iglesia en esta área en el futuro, por lo que su contribución es muy importante.

What is your greatest concern in life today? ¿Cual es su mayor preocupación en estos momentos?
_____
_____

What would you like the Church to do about your concern? ¿Cómo quisiera que la Iglesia reaccionara ante esa preocupación? _____
_____

Below are listed several groups of concerns and issues regarding worship, family life, education, etc. In the left hand column, please indicate how important each concern is to you, where 1 represents "very important" and 5 represents "not important." In the right hand column, please indicate how well the Catholic Church is meeting each concern or issue, where 1 represents "very well" and 5 represents "very poorly." Be sure to answer both questions. Please mark your answers with an (x). If you are unable to answer a question, or unsure of an answer, leave it blank.

A continuación aparece una lista de preocupaciones y asuntos relativos al culto, a la vida familiar, a la educación, etc. En la columna de la izquierda, haga el favor de marcar qué importancia tiene para usted cada tema. Use una escala del uno al cinco, donde el (1) significa que "es muy importante" y el (5) que "no es importante." En la columna de la derecha, haga el favor de marcar cómo está la Iglesia respondiendo a esas necesidades. Use una escala del uno al cinco, donde el (1) significa "muy bien" y el (5) significa "muy mal." Asegúrese de indicar sus respuestas en las dos columnas. Use una (x) para marcar sus respuestas. Si no puede contestar una pregunta, déjela en blanco.

How important is each of these to you?

¿Cuán importante es cada uno de éstos para usted?

muy _____ no muy
very _____ not very

How well is the Church meeting these needs
in your community?

¿Cómo está la Iglesia respondiendo a estas necesidad es
en su comunidad?

muy bien _____ muy mal
very well _____ very poorly

WORSHIP CONCERNS/PREOCUPACIONES SOBRE EL CULTO

1. (1) (2) (3) (4) (5)	Quality of homilies (sermons) La calidad de las homilías (sermones)	2. (1) (2) (3) (4) (5)
3. (1) (2) (3) (4) (5)	Declining church attendance La disminución en la asistencia a la Iglesiaa	4. (1) (2) (3) (4) (5)
5. (1) (2) (3) (4) (5)	Use of the sacrament of reconciliation (Confession) El uso del sacramento de reconciliación (la confesión)	6. (1) (2) (3) (4) (5)
7. (1) (2) (3) (4) (5)	Involvement of the laity in liturgy (Mass) El papel del laico en la liturgia (la Misa)	8. (1) (2) (3) (4) (5)
9. (1) (2) (3) (4) (5)	Promoting social justice through liturgy La promoción de la justicia social por medio de la liturgia	10. (1) (2) (3) (4) (5)
11. (1) (2) (3) (4) (5)	Meaningfulness of Sunday Eucharist La importancia de la Misa del Domingo	12. (1) (2) (3) (4) (5)
13. (1) (2) (3) (4) (5)	Use of devotional practices (novenas/rosaries) El uso de las devociones religiosas (novenas/rosario)	14. (1) (2) (3) (4) (5)

What other worship concerns do you believe the Church should be addressing? ¿Qué otras preocupaciones referentes al culto piensa usted que la Iglesai debe considerar? _____

How important is each of these to you?	How well is the Church meeting these needs in your community?
¿Cuán importante es cada uno de éstos para usted?	¿Cómo está la Iglasia respondiendo a estas necesidades en su comunidad?
muy _____ no muy	muy bien _____ muy mal
very _____ not very	very well _____ very poorly

SOCIAL CONCERNS/PREOCUPACIONES SOCIALES

15. (1) (2) (3) (4) (5) Involvement in war and peace issues   16. (1) (2) (3) (4) (5)
El papel de la Iglesia en cuestiones de la guerra o la paz

17. (1) (2) (3) (4) (5) Addressing unemployment, health care, housing   18. (1) (2) (3) (4) (5)
Ocuparse de problemas de desempleo, cuidados médicos y la vivienda

19. (1) (2) (3) (4) (5) Concerns about alcohol and drug abuse   20. (1) (2) (3) (4) (5)
Problemas causados por las bebidas alcohólicas y las droga

21. (1) (2) (3) (4) (5) Church's involvement in pregnancy, abortion, child abuse,   22. (1) (2) (3) (4) (5)
violence and other life issues
El papel de la Iglesia en cuestiones de embarazos, del aborto, del abuso de niños y de otros asuntos relativos a la vida

23. (1) (2) (3) (4) (5) Protecting the human rights of gay and lesbian persons   24. (1) (2) (3) (4) (5)
Proteger los derechos humanos de las personas homosexuales

25. (1) (2) (3) (4) (5) Involvement in crime and safety issues   26. (1) (2) (3) (4) (5)
El papel de la Iglesia en cuestiones relativas al crimen y la seguridad

27. (1) (2) (3) (4) (5) Promoting equality and justice for minorities   28. (1) (2) (3) (4) (5)
Promover la igualdad y la justicia para minorías

What other social concerns do you believe the Church should be addressing? ¿Qué otras preocupaciones sociales piensa usted que la Iglesia debe considerar? _____

EDUCATION CONCERNS/PREOCUPACIONES SOBRE LA EDUCACION

29. (1) (2) (3) (4) (5) Church's presence on college campuses   30. (1) (2) (3) (4) (5)
La presencia de la Iglesia en las universidades

31. (1) (2) (3) (4) (5) Financing Catholic schools   32. (1) (2) (3) (4) (5)
Financiar las escuelas Católicas

33. (1) (2) (3) (4) (5) Lifelong religious education from childhood through adulthood   34. (1) (2) (3) (4) (5)
La educación religiosa (niños y adultos)

35. (1) (2) (3) (4) (5) Sacramental preparation programs   36. (1) (2) (3) (4) (5)
La preparación para los sacramentos

37. (1) (2) (3) (4) (5) Interparish education programs   38. (1) (2) (3) (4) (5)
Programas interparroquiales de educación

39. (1) (2) (3) (4) (5) Bible study programs   40. (1) (2) (3) (4) (5)
Programas para el estudio de la Biblia

What other education concerns do you believe the Church should be addressing? ¿Qué otras preocupaciones relativas a la educación piensa usted que la Iglesia debe considerar? _____

MINISTRY CONCERNS/PREOCUPACIONES SOBRE LOS MINISTERIOS

41. (1) (2) (3) (4) (5) Education and training of laity for parish ministry and leadership   42. (1) (2) (3) (4) (5)
Educación y entrenamiento de líderes parroquiales laicos

43. (1) (2) (3) (4) (5) Encouraging Church vocations   44. (1) (2) (3) (4) (5)
Promover las vocaciones

45. (1) (2) (3) (4) (5) Financial compensation for those in ministry   46. (1) (2) (3) (4) (5)
Compensación financiera de las personas dedicadas al ministerio

47. (1) (2) (3) (4) (5) Deacons working in church ministries   48. (1) (2) (3) (4) (5)
Los diáconos en el ministerio de la Iglesia

49. (1) (2) (3) (4) (5) Training for religious education teachers   50. (1) (2) (3) (4) (5)
Entrenamiento para maestros de religión

51. (1) (2) (3) (4) (5) Women's participation in ministry   52. (1) (2) (3) (4) (5)
Promoción de la mujer en el ministerio

What other ministry concerns do you believe the Church should be addressing? ¿Qué otras preocupaciones sobre los ministerios piensa usted que la Iglesia debe considerar? _____

How important is each of these to you?

How well is the Church meeting these needs in your community?

¿Cuán importante es cada uno de éstos para usted?

¿Cómo está la Iglesia respondiendo a estas necesidades en su comunidad?

muy _____ no muy

muy bien _____ muy mal

very _____ not very

very well _____ very poorly

FAMILY LIFE CONCERNS/PREOCUPACIONES SOBRE LA VIDA FAMILIAR

53. (1) (2) (3) (4) (5)　Maintaining and enriching Christian marriage and family life　54. (1) (2) (3) (4) (5)
Mantener y enriquecer los matrimonios Cristianos y la vida familiar

55. (1) (2) (3) (4) (5)　Providing day-care and after-school care　56. (1) (2) (3) (4) (5)
Proveer el cuidado de los niños de día y después de la escuela

57. (1) (2) (3) (4) (5)　Helping the elderly and the families who care for them　58. (1) (2) (3) (4) (5)
Ayudar a los ancianos y las familias que los cuidan

59. (1) (2) (3) (4) (5)　Helping divorced and separated Catholics　60. (1) (2) (3) (4) (5)
Ayudar a los Católicos divorciados o separados

61. (1) (2) (3) (4) (5)　Concerns for single parents with children　62. (1) (2) (3) (4) (5)
Ayudar a los padres de familia solteros

63. (1) (2) (3) (4) (5)　Serving the needs of single adults　64. (1) (2) (3) (4) (5)
Ocuparse de las necesidades de las personas solteras

65. (1) (2) (3) (4) (5)　Addressing the needs of youth and young adults　66. (1) (2) (3) (4) (5)
Ocuparse de las necesidades de los jóvenes

What other family life concerns do you believe the Church should be addressing? ¿Qué otras preocupaciones relativas a la vida familiar piensa usted que la Iglesia debe considerar? _____

PARISH LIFE CONCERNS/PREOCUPACIONES SOBRE LA VIDA PARROQUIAL

67. (1) (2) (3) (4) (5)　Building up the parish as a community　68. (1) (2) (3) (4) (5)
Desarollar la parroquia como una verdadera communidad

69. (1) (2) (3) (4) (5)　Planning and management of Church money,
personnel and buildings　70. (1) (2) (3) (4) (5)
Planificación y administración del dinero,
del personal y de los edificios de la Iglesia

71. (1) (2) (3) (4) (5)　Effective parish councils and parish leadership　72. (1) (2) (3) (4) (5)
Consejos parroquiales eficaces y el liderato de la parroquia

73. (1) (2) (3) (4) (5)　Parish societies and organizations　74. (1) (2) (3) (4) (5)
Sociedades y organizaciones parroquiales

75. (1) (2) (3) (4) (5)　Effective parish communications　76. (1) (2) (3) (4) (5)
Comunicaciones parroquiales eficaces

77. (1) (2) (3) (4) (5)　Relationship between pastor and parish staff　78. (1) (2) (3) (4) (5)
Relaciones entre el párroco y el personal de la parroquia

What other parish life concerns do you believe the Church should be addressing? ¿Qué otras preocupaciones sobre la vida parroquial piensa usted que la Iglesia debe considerar? _____

EVANGELIZATION/EVANGELIZACION

79. (1) (2) (3) (4) (5)　Use of TV, radio and newspapers to spread the Gospel　80. (1) (2) (3) (4) (5)
El uso de la radio y la televisión para evangelizar

81. (1) (2) (3) (4) (5)　Outreach to inactive Catholics　82. (1) (2) (3) (4) (5)
Atraer a los Católicos inactivos

83. (1) (2) (3) (4) (5)　Raising missionary awareness at parish level　84. (1) (2) (3) (4) (5)
Despertar la conciencia misionera a nivel parroquial

85. (1) (2) (3) (4) (5)　Working towards unity with other Christian Churches　86. (1) (2) (3) (4) (5)
Tratar de obtener la unión con otros Iglesias Cristianas

87. (1) (2) (3) (4) (5)　Creating opportunities for lay people to spread the Gospel　88. (1) (2) (3) (4) (5)
Crear oportunidades para que los laicos puedan propagar el evangelio

What other evangelization concerns do you believe the Church should be addressing? ¿Qué otras preocupaciones sobre la evangelización piensa usted que la Iglesia debe considerar? _____

In your opinion, what is the most important concern facing the Church today? En us opinión, ¿cuál es el mayor problema que confronta la Iglesia en la actualidad? _____

Please fill in this background information about yourself.

Le agradeceremos que dé estas informaciones generales sobre su persona.

A. Are you ( ) Male   ( ) Female

A. ¿Es usted ( ) Hombre ( ) Mujer?

B. Which category comes closest to your age?
( ) under 18 ( ) 18-24 ( ) 25-34 ( ) 35-44
( ) 45-54 ( ) 55-64 ( ) 65 and older

B. ¿Qué categoría se acerca más a su edad?
( ) menor de 18 ( ) 18-24 ( ) 25-34 ( ) 35-44
( ) 45-54 ( ) 55-64 ( ) 65 ó mayor

C. Are you ( ) Married ( ) Single ( ) Widowed
( ) Divorced/Separated?

C. ¿Es usted ( ) Casado ( ) Soltero ( ) Viudo
( ) Divorciado o Separado?

D. Are you ( ) Asian ( ) African American
( ) American Indian ( ) Hispanic ( ) White (not of Hispanic origin) ( ) Other [specify _____]

D. ¿Es usted ( ) Asiático ( ) Indio Americano
( ) Africano Americano ( ) Hispano ( ) Blanco (no de origen hispano) ( ) Otro [especifique ____]?

E. What level of school have you completed?
( ) 1-8 [elementary] ( ) 9-12 [high school]
( ) 13-16 [college] ( ) 16+ [graduate school]

E. ¿Qué nivel de estudios ha terminado?
( ) 1-8 [primaria] ( ) 9-12 [secundaria]
( ) 13-16 [universidad] ( ) 16+ [maestría, doctorado, etc.]

F. How often did you join your community for Mass in the last 6 months? ( ) More than once a week
( ) Every Sunday ( ) Once or twice a month
( ) Just a few times in the past 6 months ( ) Not at all

F. ¿Cuántas veces asistió a la Misa en los últimos 6 meses? ( ) Más de una vez a la semana
( ) Todos los domingos ( ) Una o dos veces al mes
( ) Pocas veces en los últimos 6 meses ( ) No he ido

G. How would you describe your feelings towards the Catholic Church?: ( ) Very close and comfortable
( ) Fairly close ( ) Not close ( ) Alienated from the Church ( ) Angry with the Church

G. ¿Cómo describiría sus sentimientos hacia la Iglesia Católica? ( ) Muy satisfecho ( ) Bastante satisfecho
( ) Insatisfecho ( ) Alejado de Iglesia
( ) Enfurecido

H. You are a: ( ) Brother ( ) Deacon ( ) Layperson
( ) Priest ( ) Sister

H. Usted es: ( ) Hermano ( ) Diácono ( ) Laico
( ) Sacerdote ( ) Hermana

I. Have you held a position in the Catholic Church within the past 2 years [paid or volunteer]?:
( ) No involvement ( ) Parish Council member
( ) Parish employee ( ) Social ministry involvement
( ) Liturgical ministry ( ) Christian education teacher ( ) Parochial school employee
( ) Parish society or organization member
( ) Parish committee member
( ) Other [specify] _____

I. ¿Ha desempeñado algún trabajo en la Iglesia Católica en los últimos dos años [remunerado o voluntario]? ( ) Ninguno ( ) Miembro del Consejo Parroquial ( ) Empleado de la parroquia
( ) Ministerio Social ( ) Ministerio Litúrgico
( ) Maestro de religión ( ) Empleado de escuela parroquial ( ) Miembro de alquna sociedad u organización parroquial ( ) Miembro de un Comité Parroquial ( ) Otro [especifique]_____

J. If you have children in school, do they attend:
( ) Catholic school ( ) Public school
( ) Private school

J. Si tiene hijos en la escuela, ¿van a una:
( ) Escuela católica ( ) Escuela pública
( ) Escuela privada?

K. If you have children in school, do they attend religious education classes? ( ) Yes ( ) No

K. Si tiene hijos en la escuela, ¿asisten a las clases de educación religiosa? ( ) Sí ( ) No

L. To what parish or community do you belong? _____

L. ¿A qué parroquia o comunidad pertenece? _____

What is your zip code? _____

M. ¿Cuál es su área postal? _____

Thank you for taking the time to complete this survey!

!Gracias por haber llenado este cuestionario!

If you would like additional copies of this survey or a copy in another language, contact your parish or telephone (716) 328-3210 or 1-800-388-7177, x352 or x351.
You may return your completed survey to your parish or to the following address by April 26, 1991:

Si desea recibir copias adicionales de este cuestionario póngase en contacto con su parroquia or llame al teléfono (716) 328-3210 ó 1-800-388-7177, extensión 352 ó extensión 351.
Después de llenar el cuestionario, lo puede devolver a su parroquia o a la dirección siguiente antes del 26 de abril, 1991:

Synod Office • Diocese of Rochester • 1150 Buffalo Road • Rochester, N.Y. 14624

Notes

Introduction

1. Michael D. Shook and Jeffrey D. Meyer, *Legal Briefs: Hundreds of Entertaining Facts, Amusing Anecdotes, Odd Laws and Humorous Quotations about Lawyers and the Law* (New York: Macmillan, 1995), p. 96.

2. Philip K. Howard, *The Death of Common Sense: How Law Is Suffocating America* (New York: Random House, 1994).

3. Ibid., p. 4.

4. Ibid., p. 5.

5. Ibid., p. 11.

6. Christopher Mooney, *Public Virtue: Law and the Social Character of Religion* (Notre Dame: University of Notre Dame Press, 1986), p. 78.

7. For some recent works that present comprehensive overviews of the *Code of Canon Law*, see James A. Coriden, *An Introduction to Canon Law* (New York: Paulist Press, 1991); Jordan F. Hite and Daniel J. Ward, *Readings, Cases, Materials in Canon Law: A Textbook for Ministerial Students*, rev. ed. (Collegeville: Liturgical Press, 1990); John Huels, *The Pastoral Companion: A Canon Law Handbook for Catholic Ministry*, 2d ed. (Quincy, Ill.: Franciscan Press, 1995).

8. On October 18, 1990, Pope John Paul II promulgated the *Codex Canonum Ecclesiarum Orientalium* (Code of Canons of the Eastern Churches), the common law for the Eastern Churches.

9. See, for example, *Lumen Gentium*, no. 9: "Established by Christ as a communion of life, love and truth, it [the Church] is taken up by him also as the instrument for the salvation of all; as the light of the world and the salt of the earth (cf. Matt. 13–16) it is sent forth into the whole world." *Vatican Council II: The Conciliar and Post-Conciliar Documents*, ed. Austin Flannery (New York: Costello, 1975), p. 360.

10. Donald Heintschel, ". . . A New Way of Thinking," *The Jurist* 44 (1984), pp. 41–47.

11. Daniel Stevick, "A Theological View of the Place of Law in the Church: An Episcopalian Perspective," *The Jurist* 42 (1982), p. 4.

12. See for example, *Lumen Gentium*, no. 3: "The Church—that is the kingdom of Christ already present in mystery—grows visibly through the power of God in the world" (Flannery, *Documents*, p. 351).

13. Ladislaus Örsy, "Integrated Interpretation: Or, the Role of Theology in the Interpretation of Canon Law," *Studia Canonica* 22 (1988), p. 252.

14. Ibid.

Chapter One

1. All Scripture quotations, unless otherwise noted, are from *The Jerusalem Bible* (Garden City: Doubleday, 1985).

2. Frank Gorman, Jr., "When Law Becomes Gospel: Matthew's Transformed Torah," *Listening* 24 (1989), p. 228.

3. Ibid.

4. Ibid., p. 230.

5. Harold Berman, *The Interaction of Law and Religion* (New York: Abingdon Press, 1974), p. 52.

6. Ibid., p. 53.

7. Richard Cunningham, "Back to the Future," *Canon Law Society of America Proceedings* 52 (1990), p. 2.

8. Ibid.

9. James Brundage, *Medieval Canon Law* (New York: Longman, 1995), pp. 11–13.

10. Coriden, *Introduction to Canon Law*, p. 27.

11. "The instrument which the Code is fully corresponds to the nature of the Church, especially as it is proposed by the teaching of the Second Vatican Council in general and in a particular way by its ecclesiological teaching. Indeed, in a certain sense this new Code could be understood as a great effort to translate this same conciliar doctrine and ecclesiology into *canonical* language. If, however, it is impossible to translate perfectly into *canonical* language the conciliar image of the Church, nevertheless the Code must always be referred to this image as the primary pattern whose outline the Code ought to express insofar as it can by its very nature" (Apostolic Constitution, *Sacrae Disciplinae Leges*, in *Code of Canon Law, Latin-English Edition* [Washington, D.C.: Canon Law Society of America, 1983], xiv, emphasis added).

Chapter Two

1. "Ecclesiastical laws are to be understood in accord with the proper meaning of the words, considered in their text and context. If the meaning remains doubtful and obscure recourse is to be taken to parallel passages if

such exist, to the purpose and circumstances of the law, and to the *mind of the legislator*"(emphasis added).

2. By the time of Boniface VIII (1294–1303), the popes had drastically reduced their responsibilities as judges for the numerous cases from throughout Christendom that had been appealed to them for a decision. In order to deal with routine judicial business, special hearing officers were appointed by the popes. These officials began conducting legal hearings in a special round courtroom within the papal palace. "The shape of this room, perhaps coupled with the auditors' practice of taking turns in hearing cases, suggested the nickname of 'the wheel' (rota) for the court itself" (Brundage, *Medieval Canon Law*, pp. 125–26).

3. Pope Paul VI, "Justice in Service of the Gospel," in William Woestman, ed., *Papal Allocutions to the Roman Rota, 1939–1994* (Ottawa: St. Paul University, 1994), p. 148.

4. Ibid., p. 138.

5. Ibid., p. 141.

6. Ibid.

7. Ibid., p. 141.

8. Pope Paul VI, "Necessity of Canon Law, Its Pastoral Nature," in ibid., p. 113.

9. Ibid., p. 114.

10. Ibid.

11. Ibid., p. 142.

12. Ibid., p. 129.

13. Ibid., p. 118.

14. Ibid., p. 120.

15. Ibid., p. 122.

16. Pope Paul VI, "Judicial Authority in the Contemporary Church," in ibid., p. 109.

17. Ibid., p. 110.

18. Pope Paul VI, "Freedom of the Children of God and the Necessity of Law," in ibid., p. 98.

19. Ibid., p. 99.

20. Ibid.

21. Pope John Paul II, "The Church and Protection of Fundamental Human Rights," in ibid., p. 153.

22. Ibid., p. 154.

23. Ibid., pp. 209–13.

24. Ibid., p. 209.

25. Ibid., p. 210.

26. Ibid., p. 211.

27. John Paul II, "Interpret Law in the Light of Tradition," in ibid., p. 223.

28. Ibid., p. 229.

Chapter Three

1. *Gaudium et Spes,* 29, in Flannery, *Documents,* p. 929.

2. For an exploration of the development of the Roman Catholic human rights tradition, see, for example, Alfred Henelly and John Langan, eds., *Human Rights in the Americas: The Struggle for Consensus* (Washington, D.C.: Georgetown University Press, 1982); David O'Brien and Thomas Shannon, eds., *Renewing the Earth: Catholic Documents on Peace, Justice and Liberation* (Garden City: Image Books, 1977); David Hollenbach, *Claims and Conflicts: Retrieving and Renewing the Catholic Human Rights Tradition* (New York: Paulist Press, 1979).

3. Raymond Corrigan, *The Church and the Nineteenth Century* (Milwaukee: Bruce, 1948), p. 242.

4. Pope Leo XIII, *On the Condition of the Working Classes, Rerum Novarum* (Boston: St. Paul Editions, 1942), p. 36.

5. Ibid., p. 36.

6. Pope John XXIII, *Peace on Earth, Pacem in Terris* (Boston: St. Paul Editions, 1963), pp. 9, 11, 12.

7. Ibid., p. 12.

8. Ibid., p. 9.

9. Pope John Paul II, *Redemptor Hominis, Redeemer of Man* (Ottawa: Canadian Conference of Catholic Bishops, 1979), p. 28.

10. "Baptismate homo constituitur in Ecclesia Christi persona cum omnibus christianorum iuribus et officiis, nisi, ad iura quod attinet, obstet obex, ecclesiasticae communionis vinculum impediens, vel lata ab Ecclesia censura." (By virtue of Baptism, one becomes a person in the Church of Christ with all the rights and obligations of a Christian unless, in regards to rights, there is an obstacle which impedes the bond of ecclesiastical communion or a censure imposed by the Church.)

11. "The Christian faithful are those who, inasmuch as they have been incorporated in Christ through baptism, have been constituted as the people of God" (canon 204 §1).

12. "Principles Which Govern the Revision of the Code of Canon Law," translation in Hite and Ward, *Readings, Cases, Materials in Canon Law,* p. 86.

13. Ibid., p. 90.

14. Ibid.

15. Ibid.

16. Ibid.

17. Ibid., p. 91.

18. James A. Coriden, "A Challenge: Making the Rights Real," *The Jurist* 45 (1985), p. 4.

19. A controversial document prepared during the course of drafting the 1983 code by a commission independent of the code commission. It was an attempt to provide a "fundamental law" or "constitution" for the Church, but it was never promulgated. However, much of its content, especially in regards to rights and obligations, has been included in the code.

20. "[T]he Code of Canon Law is extremely necessary for the Church . . . in order that the mutual relations of the faithful may be regulated according to justice based on charity, with the rights of individuals guaranteed and well defined" (*Code of Canon Law, Latin-English Edition*, xv).

21. James Provost, "Ecclesial Rights," *Canon Law Society Proceedings* 44 (1982), p. 42.

22. Terrence Grant, "Social Justice in the 1983 Code of Canon Law: An Examination of Selected Canons," *The Jurist* 49 (1989), p. 124.

23. Waltar Kasper, "The Theological Foundation of Human Rights," *The Jurist* 50 (1990), p. 149.

24. Ibid., p. 166.

Chapter Four

1. *Gaudium et Spes*, 26, in Flannery, *Documents*, p. 927. Emphasis added.

2. Sacred Congregation for Religious, *Sedes Sapientiae and the General Statutes*, 2d ed. (Washington, D.C.: Catholic University of America Press, 1957).

3. Pope Pius XII, "Iis qui interfuerunt Conventui XIII Societatis internationalis 'de Psychologie appliquée,'" *The Pope Speaks* 5 (1958), p. 15.

4. Ibid.

5. Anne Anastasi, "Psychological Testing and Privacy," in William Christian Bier, *Privacy: A Vanishing Value?* (New York: Fordham University Press, 1980), p. 51.

6. John Ford, *Religious Superiors, Subjects, and Psychiatrists* (Westminster, Md.: Newman Press, 1963), p. 45.

7. Ibid.

8. Elissa Rinere, "The Individual's Right to Confidentiality," *Bulletin on Religious Law* 11 (1995), p. 3.

9. William Christian Bier, "Psychological Tests and Psychic Privacy," *Catholic Theological Society of America Proceedings* 17 (1962), p. 68.

10. Rinere, "Right to Confidentiality," p. 3.

11. Ibid., p. 4

12. Ibid.

13. Ibid., p. 5.

14. Ibid.

15. Ibid.

Chapter Five

1. John Paul II, "Apostolic Exhortation on the Family," *Origins* 11 (1981), p. 465.

2. In this chapter, the term "annulment" will be utilized, since it is so widely used; the common canonical expression is "declaration of nullity."

3. Thomas G. Green, "Ministering to Marital Failure," *Chicago Studies* 2 (1979), p. 329.

4. Canon 1060: "Marriage enjoys the favor of the law; consequently, when a doubt exists the validity of a marriage is to be upheld until the contrary is proven."

5. Canon 1057 §1.

6. Patrick Power, "Pastoral Role of the Tribunal," in Hugh F. Doogan, ed., *Catholic Tribunals: Marriage Annulments and Dissolutions* (Newtown, Australia: E. J. Dwyer, 1990), p. 1.

7. Elizabeth Kübler-Ross, *On Death and Dying* (New York: Macmillan, 1969).

8. Power, "Pastoral Roles," p. 2.

9. Ibid.

10. Richard Haas, "Annulment: A Personal Reflection," *America* 162 (1990), p. 499.

11. Ibid., p. 500.

12. Ibid.

13. Ibid.

14. Paula Ripple, "The Spiritual Journey of the Divorcing Catholic," in James Young, ed., *Divorce Ministry and the Marriage Tribunal* (New York: Paulist Press, 1982), p. 44.

15. Ibid.

16. Kathleen Kircher, "The Shape of Divorce Ministry Today," in Young, *Divorce Ministry,* p. 6.

17. Joseph Frederico, "Estimating Emotional Readiness for Annulment," in Young, *Divorce Ministry,* p. 48.

18. Ibid., p. 50.

19. Ibid., p. 53.

20. Ibid., pp. 55–56.

21. Haas, "Annulment," p. 500.

22. Gerald Washko, "Healing and the Annulment Process: A Perspective of a Contextual Family Therapist," in *New Catholic World* 229 (1986), p. 35.

23. Andrew McDonald, "On the Side of the Law, On the Side of the Wounded," *Origins* 25 (1995), p. 225.

Chapter Six

1. Lawrence Jennings, "A Renewed Understanding of the Diocesan Synod," *Studia Canonica* 20 (1986), p. 321.

2. Ibid., p. 323.

3. Ibid.

4. "For those who believe in Christ, who are reborn, not from corruptible seed, but from an incorruptible one through the word of the living God (cf. 1 Peter 1:23), not from flesh, but from water and the Holy Spirit (cf. John 3:5–6), are finally established as a 'chosen race, a royal priesthood, a holy nation . . . who in times past were not a people, but now are the people of God'" (1 Peter 2:9–10). (No. 9, in Flannery, *Documents,* p. 359).

5. Sacred Congregation for Bishops, *Directory on the Pastoral Ministry of Bishops* (Ottawa: Publications Service of the Canadian Catholic Conference, 1974), p. 83.

6. Ibid.

7. "The diocesan bishop is the sole legislator at a diocesan synod while the remaining members of the synod possess only a consultative vote; he alone signs the synodal declarations and decrees which can be published only through his authority." (Ibid., canon 466.)

8. "That which touches all ought to be approved by all" (*Quod omnes tangit debet ob omnibus approbari*). Reg. 29, RJ, in VI (Rule 29 in the Regula Iuris of Boniface VIII's "Sixth Book").

9. A preponderance of the legislation of the Rochester synod of 1954, typical of synods of the time, concerned regulations for clergy, such as proper clerical attire: "We condemn the practice of going to the door or to the parish office in sport shirts and the like. . . . Our priests will wear hats when travelling on the streets." (*Liber Synodalis Roffensis* [Rochester: Riley Printer, 1954], II, 11, p. 42.)

10. Matthew Clark, *Pastoral Plan, Roman Catholic Diocese of Rochester, 1995–1999* (Rochester: Rochester Catholic Press Association, 1995).

Chapter Seven

1. As quoted by James Provost, "The Nature of Rights in the Church," *Canon Law Society of America Proceedings* 53 (1991), p. 13.

2. Neighboring diocesan churches are grouped together into an ecclesiastical province, one of which is designated as an "archdiocese" whose bishop is the "metropolitan" of the province, with certain limited responsibilities in regards to the neighboring dioceses. A "metropolitan tribunal" is the tribunal of an archdiocese.

3. Leonard Swidler and Herbert O'Brien, eds., *A Catholic Bill of Rights* (Kansas City, Mo.: Sheed and Ward, 1988), p. 66.

4. Mooney, *Public Virtue*, p. 96.

5. Ricardo Bass, "Due Process: Conciliation and Arbitration," *Canon Law Society of America Proceedings* 53 (1991), p. 63.

6. Ibid., p. 64.

7. Ibid., p. 63.

8. For an overview of the efforts of the Canon Law Society of America to promote due process procedures in the dioceses of the United States over the last several years, see John Beal, "On Due Process: The Third Decade," in *Protection of Rights of Persons in the Church: Revised Report of the Canon Law Society of America* (Washington, D.C.: Canon Law Society of America, 1991), pp. 1–11.

9. Bass, "Due Process," p. 75.

10. James A. Coriden, "Alternative Dispute Resolution in the Church," *Canon Law Society of America Proceedings* 48 (1986) pp. 64–65.

11. Ibid., p. 65.

12. A formal canonical procedure, in which a demand is made to the superior of the originator of a decree or nonjudicial decision that a review be made of the original decree or decision. Such a demand must follow strict procedures and time limits, as defined in canon law.

13. Coriden, "Alternative Dispute Resolution," p. 74.

14. Ibid., p. 75.

15. Ibid., p. 77.

Epilogue

1. Howard, *Death of Common Sense*, p. 38.

2. Ibid., p. 49.

3. Ibid.

4. Mooney, *Public Virtue*, p. 75.

5. Keith Egan, "The Call of the Laity to a Spirituality of Discipleship," *The Jurist* 47 (1987), p. 84.

6. Ibid., p. 79.

7. John Sheets, "Ministry, Spirituality, and the Canon Lawyer," *Studia Canonica* 12 (1978), p. 57.

8. Ibid., p. 66.

9. Ibid., p. 68.

Bibliography

Primary Sources

Clark, Matthew. *Pastoral Plan, Roman Catholic Diocese of Rochester, 1995–1999.* Rochester: Rochester Catholic Press Association, 1995.

Code of Canon Law, Latin-English Edition. Translation prepared under the auspices of the Canon Law Society of America. Washington, D.C.: Canon Law Society of America, 1983.

Flannery, Austin, ed. *Vatican Council II: The Conciliar and Post-Conciliar Documents.* New York: Costello, 1975.

John XXIII. *Peace on Earth, Pacem in Terris.* Boston: St. Paul Editions, 1963.

John Paul II. "Apostolic Exhortation on the Family," *Origins* 11 (1981), pp. 437–68.

———. *Redemptor Hominis, Redeemer of Man.* Ottawa: Canadian Conference of Catholic Bishops, 1979.

Leo XIII. *On the Condition of the Working Class, Rerum Novarum.* Boston: St. Paul Editions, 1942.

Liber Synodalis Roffensis. Rochester: Riley Printer, 1954.

Pius XII. "Iis qui interfuerunt Conventui XIII Societatis internationalis 'de Psychologie appliquée'." *The Pope Speaks* 5 (1958), pp. 7–20.

Sacred Congregation for Bishops. *Directory on the Pastoral Ministry of Bishops.* Ottawa: Publications Service of the Canadian Catholic Conference, 1974.

Sacred Congregation for Religious, *Sedes Sapientiae and the General Statutes.* 2d ed. Washington, D.C.: Catholic University of America Press, 1957.

Woestman, William, ed. *Papal Allocutions to the Roman Rota, 1939–1994.* Ottawa: Faculty of Canon Law, St. Paul University, 1994.

Works Consulted

Anastasi, Anne. "Psychological Testing and Privacy." In William Christian Bier, *Privacy: A Vanishing Value?* New York: Fordham University Press, 1980, pp. 348–58.

Bass, Ricardo. "Due Process: Conciliation and Arbitration." *Canon Law Society of America Proceedings* 53 (1991), pp. 63–76.

Beal, J., "On Due Process: The Third Decade." In *Protection of Rights of Persons in the Church: Revised Report of the Canon Law Society of America.* Washington, D.C.: Canon Law Society of America, 1991, pp. 1–11.

Berman, Harold. *The Interaction of Law and Religion.* New York: Abingdon Press, 1974.

Bier, William Christian. "Psychological Tests and Privacy." *Catholic Theological Society of America Proceedings* 17 (1962), pp. 161–79.

Brundage, James. *Medieval Canon Law.* New York: Longman, 1995.

Coriden, James A. "A Challenge: Making the Rights Real." *The Jurist* 45 (1985), pp. 1–23.

———. "Alternative Dispute Resolution in the Church." *Canon Law Society of America Proceedings* 48 (1986), pp. 61–82.

———. *An Introduction to Canon Law.* New York: Paulist Press, 1991.

Corrigan, Raymond. *The Church and the Nineteenth Century.* Milwaukee: Bruce, 1948.

Cunningham, Richard. "Back to the Future." *Canon Law Society of America Proceedings* 52 (1990), pp. 1–10.

Doogan, Hugh F., ed. *Catholic Tribunals: Marriage Annulments and Dissolution.* Newtown, Australia: E. J. Dwyer, 1990.

Egan, Keith. "The Call of the Laity to a Spirituality of Discipleship." *The Jurist* 47 (1987), pp. 71–85.

Ford, John. *Religious Superiors, Subjects, and Psychiatrists.* Westminster, Md.: Newman Press, 1963.

Gorman, Frank, Jr. "When Law Becomes Gospel: Matthew's Transformed Torah." *Listening* 24 (1989), pp. 227–40.

Grant, Terrence. "Social Justice in the 1983 Code of Canon Law: An Examination of Selected Canons." *The Jurist* 49 (1989), pp. 112–45.

Green, Thomas G. "Ministering to Marital Failure." *Chicago Studies* 2 (1979), pp. 327–44.

Haas, Richard. "Annulment: A Personal Reflection." *America* 162 (1990), pp. 499–501.

Heintschel, Donald. ". . . A New Way of Thinking." *The Jurist* 44 (1984), pp. 41–47.

Henelly, Alfred, and John Langan, eds. *Human Rights in the Americas: The Struggle for Consensus.* Washington, D.C.: Georgetown University Press, 1982.

Hite, Jordan F., and Daniel J. Ward. *Readings, Cases, Materials in Canon Law: A Textbook for Ministerial Students.* Rev. ed. Collegeville: Liturgical Press, 1990.

Hollenbach, David. *Claims and Conflicts: Retrieving and Renewing the Catholic Human Rights Tradition.* New York: Paulist Press, 1979.

Howard, Philip K. *The Death of Common Sense: How Law Is Suffocating America.* New York: Random House, 1994.

Huels, John. *The Pastoral Companion: A Canon Law Handbook for Catholic Ministry.* 2d ed. Quincy, Ill.: Franciscan Press, 1995.

Ioppolo, Donna Krier, Marie Breitenbeck, Elissa Rinere, and Ronald Stake. *Confidentiality in the United States: A Legal and Canonical Study.* Washington, D.C.: Canon Law Society of America, 1988.

Jennings, Lawrence. "A Renewed Understanding of the Diocesan Synod." *Studia Canonica* 20 (1986), pp. 319–54.

Kasper, Waltar. "The Theological Foundation of Human Rights." *The Jurist* 50 (1990), pp. 148–66.

Kübler-Ross, Elizabeth. *On Death and Dying.* New York: Macmillan, 1969.

McDonald, Andrew. "On the Side of the Law, On the Side of the Wounded." *Origins* 25 (1995), pp. 224–25.

Mooney, Christopher. *Public Virtue: Law and the Social Character of Religion.* Notre Dame: University of Notre Dame Press, 1986.

O'Brien, David, and Thomas Shannon, eds. *Renewing the Earth: Catholic Documents on Peace, Justice, and Liberation.* Garden City, N.Y.: Image Books, 1977.

Örsy, Ladislaus. "Integrated Interpretation: Or, The Role of Theology in the Interpretation of Canon Law." *Studia Canonica* 22 (1988), pp. 245–64.

Provost, James. "Ecclesial Rights." *Canon Law Society of America Proceedings* 44 (1982), pp. 41–62.

———. "The Nature of Rights in the Church." *Canon Law Society of America Proceedings* 53 (1991), pp. 1–18.

Rinere, Elissa. "The Individual's Right to Confidentiality." *Bulletin on Religious Law* 11 (1995), pp. 1–6.

Sheets, John. "Ministry, Spirituality, and the Canon Lawyer." *Studia Canonica* 12 (1978), pp. 57–71.

Shook, Michael D., and Jeffrey D. Meyer. *Legal Briefs: Hundreds of Entertaining Facts, Amusing Anecdotes, Odd Laws and Humorous Quotations about Lawyers and the Law.* New York: Macmillan, 1995.

Stevick, Daniel. "A Theological View of the Place of Law in the Church: An Episcopalian Perspective." *The Jurist* 42 (1982), pp. 1–13.

Swidler, Leonard, and Herbert O'Brien, eds. *A Catholic Bill of Rights.* Kansas City, Mo.: Sheed and Ward, 1988.

Washko, Gerald. "Healing and the Annulment Process: A Perspective of a Contextual Family Therapist." *New Catholic World* 229 (1986), pp. 32–36.

Young, James, ed. *Divorce Ministry and the Marriage Tribunal.* New York: Paulist Press, 1982.

Index

Abelard, Peter, 12

administration. *See* personnel issues

Alternative Dispute Resolution (ADR) model, 68–70

Anastasi, Anne, 39

annulment, 45–53; codification of, 5; defined, 46; and reconciliation, 5, 45, 47, 48–49, 52

"Apostolic Exhortation on the Family" (John Paul II), 45

arbitration, 67–68

Augustine, Saint, 72

authority: biblical, 18, 28, 33; ecclesial, 17; protections against arbitrariness, 18, 30, 31; as service to community, 7; subsidiarity of, 17–18

baptism, right and obligations of, x, 29, 32, 38, 45

Bass, Ricardo, 68

Berman, Harold, 11

Bernard of Clairvaux, Saint, 18

Bible, authority in, 18, 28, 33

Bible citations: Gen. 1:28, 25; Josh. 1:6–8, 9; Ps. 112[111]:4, 20; Ps. 119, 10–11; Matt. 5:17, 10; Matt. 5:19, 10; Matt. 18:15–18, 66; John 3:5–6, 85n. 4; 2 Tim. 4:8, 20; 1 Peter 1:23, 85n. 4; 1 Peter 2:9–10, 85n. 4; 1 John 1:9, 20

Bier, William Christian, 40

bishops: as civil judges, 66; and diocesan synods, 56, 57, 58; responsibilities of, 35, 36, 42–43, 58; synods of, 55–56

Boniface VIII, Pope, 13

canon law: chronological collections of, 11–12; development of, 4, 9–14; Eastern code of, 4, 14, 79n. 8; Latin code of, 4; modern conception of, 3; as pastoral, 18–20; penalties in, 21; purpose of, 3, 9, 29–30; as redeeming tool, 7–8, 22; secular influence on, 19

Canon Law Society of America, 86n. 8

canons, defined, 12

Carnelutti, Francesco, 22

Chappuis, John, 13

charity, 19

Church law. *See* canon law

civil disobedience, 11

civil law: due process in, 66; influence on canon law, 19; modern conception of, 1–3; overregulation of, 1, 2, 71; proliferation of litigation in, 2; purpose of, 9. *See also* Roman law

Clark, Bishop Matthew H., 55, 59, 60, 62–63